Creative Cloth
Doll

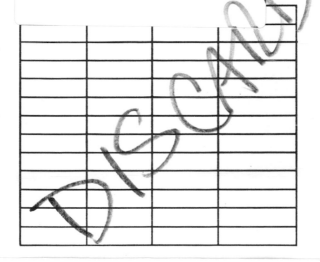

QUARRY

Creative Cloth

Doll
Beading

Designing
and Embellishing
with Beads

PATTI MEDARIS CULEA

WITH ANNE HESSE AND LAURA MCCABE

QUARRY BOOKS

First published in the United States of America by
Quarry Books, a member of
Quayside Publishing Group
33 Commercial Street
Gloucester, Massachusetts 01930-5089
Telephone: (978) 282-9590
Fax: (978) 283-2742
www.quarrybooks.com

Library of Congress Cataloging-in-Publication Data

Medaris Culea, Patti.
    Creative cloth doll beading : designing and embellishing with beads / Patti Medaris Culea, with Anne Hesse and Laura McCabe.
        p.   cm.
    ISBN-13: 978-1-59253-311-4
    ISBN-10: 1-59253-311-6
    1. Beadwork. 2. Dollmaking. 3. Cloth dolls. I. Hesse, Anne. II. McCabe, Laura. III. Title.
TT860.M43 2007
    745.592'21—dc22   2006030522
                                                                                          CIP

ISBN-13: 978-1-59253-311-4
ISBN-10: 1-59253-311-6

10 9 8 7 6 5 4 3 2 1

Design: Stephen Gleason Design
Cover Image: Allan Penn Photography
Photography: Robert Hirsch
Illustrations: Gayle Isabelle Ford, except those on pages 20–22, 27 (top left), and 28 by Judy Love
Patterns: Roberta Frauwirth
Technical Editor: Susan Huxley
Assistant Technical Editor: Katherine O. Riess

Printed in Singapore

In loving memory of
Frances Elizabeth Lefever Medaris

CONTENTS

INTRODUCTION

This is a book that begins with the smallest of art forms: the bead. Whereas dolls often stand alone and can be aloof, beads are highly social. Beads need each other—they like each other.

We all know that beads have origins that can be traced to Japan, Italy, Africa, China, the Czech Republic, and the Native Americans. There are categories of beads: natural and true. Some claim there are beads with spirits—or beads that become dysfunctional by losing either their "body" or "spirit." Goodness, that's too deep for this book. Let's instead keep it light.

Beads are not always found in traditional places. Look around your home or go to your hardware store, mailing center, or woodworking store and you'll find wonderful beads or beadlike embellishments for your doll.

Consider lowly and underappreciated washers. They spend their entire lives inside a nozzle or faucet head. They come in all sizes and would love to be used as simple, yet fun, ways to dress up a doll, quilt, or vest. Washers can be painted, wrapped in yarn, or covered with seed beads to give any project that extra touch of "cool."

This is a book about having fun. We'll do it by sharing beading techniques to create wonderful families of beads who will proudly cling to your works of art.

Two of my good friends will help you as you turn these pages. Anne Hesse is famous for her whimsical and funky bead embroidery. Laura McCabe's world sparkles with crystals. We hope you enjoy these projects and find limitless inspiration in this exploration of beading and embellishment.

—Patti Medaris Culea

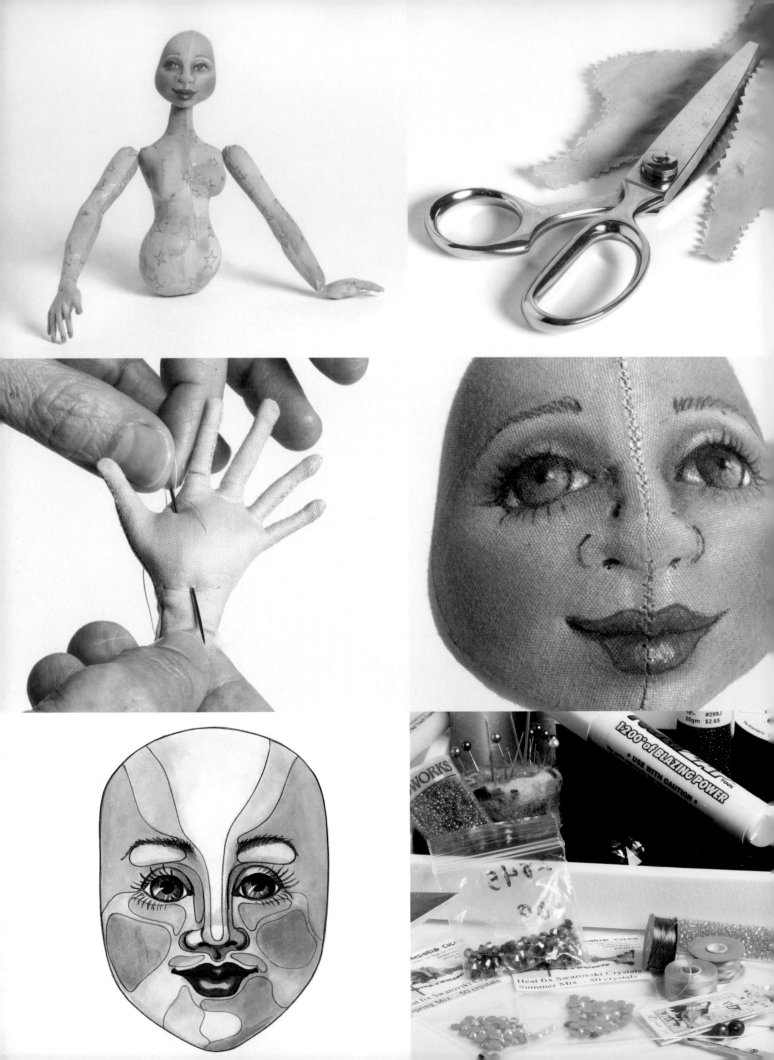

Chapter 1

Getting
Started
and
Basic Beading

Without a doll, a bead is relegated to a communal life in a bead tray. But before we address bead techniques, let's review the basics for making a doll. This chapter includes instructions for making the Basic Doll Body. Keep the doll at 18" (45.7 cm) tall. This size is just right to "draw a bead on."

Before starting a project, assemble all of your materials. The materials kits listed here include all of the essential items for creating the doll's body, the clothing, and the bead accessories.

Later in the chapter you will find explanations of beading terminology, tools, and materials. We will also cover several basic beading techniques that will be referred to in later chapters.

The Basic Body Kit

❋ Basic Body pattern pieces (page 114)

❋ ⅓ yard (0.31 m) of tan, light-colored, or batik 100% cotton fabric for the body and head

❋ mohair, Tibetan goatskin, yarn, fabric, or beads for the hair

❋ colored pencils: light or sienna brown for shading; lighter tan, beige, or flesh for highlights; white for pronounced highlights; carmine red for cheeks; light, medium, and dark for eyes; two shades of pink, red, or rose for lips

❋ fabric pens: black for the pupils and eyelashes (optional), brown for outlining all of the features, contrasting color for the eyes, red for outlining the lips and dotting the tear ducts

❋ white gel pen

❋ 6 pipe cleaners for wiring fingers

❋ stuffing such as Fairfield Poly-fil

❋ textile medium such as Createx Textile Medium or Jo Sonja's Textile Medium

❋ thread matched to fabric

❋ strong thread matched to fabric for sculpting and attaching arms, legs, and hair

❋ soft fabric eraser such as Magic Rub

❋ mechanical pencil

❋ clear plastic quilter's gridded ruler

❋ stuffing tools

❋ sewing machine

❋ turning tools such as the Itsy Bitsy Finger Turning kit or small brass tubes (see Resources, page 121)

❋ needle-nose pliers

❋ wire cutters

❋ light table (optional)

The Basic Clothing Kit

* cotton batik fabrics
* cotton print fabrics
* synthetic fabrics such as polyester organza
* silk fabrics such as chiffon, crepe de Chine, dupioni, or sand-washed charmeuse
* variegated and metallic sewing machine threads
* lace
* trims
* silk ribbons

The Basic Beading Kit

* seed beads in various colors: sizes 6, 8, 11, and 15
* size 15 charlottes in various colors
* size 11 Miyuki Delica seed beads
* accent beads: drop, lentil, flower, bugle, triangle, square, and leaf
* beading threads: Nymo, FireLine, wax

The Basic Sewing Kit

* sewing machine
* sewing machine needles: universal points in sizes 10 and 12; embroidery, metallic, and top stitch in size 12
* hand-sewing needles (sharps, milliners, quilter's basting, darners, embroidery, chenille)
* size 24 (small) tapestry needle
* variety of sewing machine presser feet, such as darning, open-toed, and zigzag
* sewing machine tools (for changing needles, oiling, and cleaning)
* seam ripper
* iron
* press cloth
* small bottle of Sewer's Aid
* extra bobbins
* straight pins
* safety pins
* pincushion
* thimble
* cutting rulers
* clear plastic quilter's gridded ruler
* measuring tape
* template plastic, card stock, or heavy paper (optional)
* rotary cutter and self-healing cutting board (optional)
* straight-edge fabric scissors
* embroidery scissors
* paper scissors
* pinking shears
* hemostats (handheld surgical clamps) or forceps
* stuffing fork
* pencil

Body made from star fabric, not clothed

THE BODY CONSTRUCTION

The pattern pieces for the Basic Body start on page 114. Do not cut out the pattern pieces before reviewing the construction steps that start below. Some pattern pieces are traced on to the fabric with a mechanical pencil, and then sewn before they are cut out: Face, Head Back, Arm, and Leg. The main body pieces are cut out in detail and then sewn together.

As you sew, backstitch at all openings. This is especially important for the neck.

Have a new needle in your sewing machine and shorten the stitch length slightly. You want a closer stitch, which will prevent the seams from splitting, plus fewer stitches are visible. On a Bernina, for example, rather than the normal 2.0, move the setting down to 1.8 (about 15 stitches per inch [2.5 cm]).

1 Trace the Face and Head onto the wrong side of the body fabric, matching the grain lines. With the fabric folded so there are two layers, machine sew seam #1 on the Face and seam #2 on the Head Back (figure a). Leave open where marked on the Head Back.

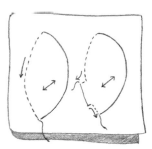

(figure a)
Sew head before cutting the fabric.

2 Cut out the head pieces using full ⅛" (3 mm) seam allowances along seam #1 and seam #2, and open each one up. Pin the pattern pieces, right sides together, at the chin and top of head, matching the seams. Machine sew all the way around along seam #3 (figure b). Clip the curves and turn the head right side out.

(figure b)
Sew front of head to back of head.

3 Fill the head with stuffing and set it aside for now.

4 Trace the Body Front onto the wrong side of the body fabric. Double the fabric and cut it out. Trace all of the darts. Flip the pattern template over when tracing on the reverse side of the body. The Body Back is a single piece. Trace this onto the wrong side of a single piece of fabric and cut it out. Trace all of the darts.

5 After you cut out the body pieces, machine sew all of the darts (figure c). Pin the two Body Front pieces right sides together and sew seam #4.

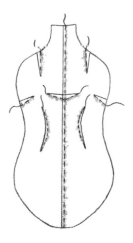

(figure c)
Sew darts on body front.

6 On the Body Back, cut along the solid line from the neck to the end of the dart (figure d). Fold the Body Back so that the right sides match. Machine sew down dart #1, leaving open where marked. (Note: For fray-free assembly, use pinking shears to trim seam allowances.)

(figure d)
Cut down the center back.

7 Pin the Body Front to the Body Back, right sides together, and machine sew all the way from the neck opening, around the body, to the other side of the neck opening. Leave the neck open at the top. As the neck is sewn, backstitch at either side of the opening.

8 Turn the body right side out and fill it firmly with stuffing. Be sure to plump up the breasts. Ladder stitch opening closed on back. Set the body aside for now.

9 Trace two arms on the wrong side of the same fabric as the body. Double the fabric, right sides together, and pin the layers together in several places. Machine sew from the opening at the wrist all the way around. Cut out, using a full ⅛" (3 mm) seam allowance, and turn. Fill the arms with stuffing from the top to the elbows and set aside.

10 Make a complete pattern piece for a leg by tracing the upper and lower leg shapes onto template plastic and then overlap and tape together the edges as marked. Trace two legs onto the wrong side of the Body fabric. Transfer the slit mark to the right side of each piece. Double the fabric, right sides together, and pin around the shapes. Sew all the way around from the opening at the feet. Cut out the legs using full ⅛" (3 mm) seam allowances, but don't turn the shape right side out yet.

11 Trace the Foot template (page 117) on to template plastic, card stock, or heavy paper. Cut this out using paper scissors. Refold the bottom of the leg and pin the center seams together on the foot, with the fabric right sides together. Lay the template you made of the foot on to the fabric foot and trace around the foot and big toe with a mechanical pencil (figure e). Sew along the traced line. Trim and then clip the curves of the seam allowances.

(figure e)
Trace and sew the foot.

12 Place the legs together with the feet facing each other and cut a slit—only on the side facing you—where marked on each leg. Turn each leg through the opening and fill both legs from the toes to the knee. To allow the legs to bend so the doll can sit, a bit of sculpting will be done with strong thread.

13 Secure the end of the thread on the seam line at the back of the knee (figure f, left). Push the needle inside the leg and come out about ¼" (6 mm) from the seam at the center front of the knee, on the front of the leg (#1) (figure f, right). To sew the knee dimple, take the needle up about ½" (1.3 cm) and push the needle into the leg (#2). Take the needle straight across and out the knee to the other side of the front of the leg about ¼" (6 mm) from the center seam (#3) and in line with the stitch just made. Take the needle down about ½" (1.3 cm) and then push the needle into the knee (#4). Come out on the other side, in line with this stitch, or into the first stitch created. Come out at this point, then take the thread around the back of the leg and back into #3. Pull the thread tightly.

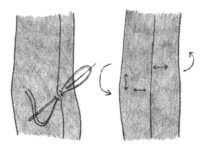

(figure f)
Left: Secure thread without a knot.
Right: Sculpt the leg.

14 The thread will sink into the back of the leg, allowing the leg to bend so that the doll can sit. Anchor the thread at the back of the knee and cut it off. Fill the upper part of the leg lightly with stuffing and sew the opening closed. Still using strong thread, sew the legs to the body starting at the side of the hip. Make sure that the slit at the top of each leg is closest to the body, so it isn't visible when the leg is attached to the body.

15 Trace two hands onto the wrong side of the body fabric. Double the fabric and pin to secure. Backstitch as you start to machine sew at the wrist. Carefully sew around the fingers. You'll need to have at least two stitches across the tips of each finger and two in between the fingers.

Tip:

It is very important to stitch exactly on the tracing lines for the hand and get those two stitches across the tips and between each finger. I always stitch my doll hands by machine with an open-toe presser foot so the pencil line is always clearly visible. The fingers need to be wide enough for a tube to fit inside when turning a finger right side out.

16 Make sure the gap between the fingers is a straight stitch, not a pivot point (V shape). Otherwise, you'll have a difficult time turning the fingers and preventing wrinkles. After sewing the entire hand with tiny stitches, cut out the hand, with a scant ⅛" (3 mm) seam allowance.

17 Using sharp scissors, cut into the inside curves between each finger. Cut to within a fabric thread of the stitching between the fingers.

18 Turning the hands is very easy if you use little brass tubes that are narrow enough to insert into a finger. Place a tube inside a finger. On the outside, gently press the brass rod against the tip of the finger and tube. The aim is to push the finger up the brass rod, not shove the rod inside the tube (figure g). Fold over the seam allowance at the tip of the finger as you do this.

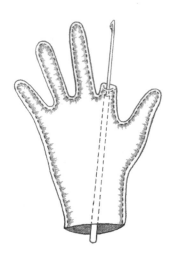

(figure g)
Use tubes to turn the fingers.

19 Gently roll the finger up the rod. This takes practice, but once you try it, it becomes easy. Repeat with the next finger, and the next, until all fingers are sitting inside the palm of the hand.

20 Once the fingers are turned, reach into the hand with a pair of hemostats and pull the entire hand right side out. Using six pipe cleaners, bend back just the tips of all of the ends. I bend the tip of each pipe cleaner at the beginning of the process so I don't forget to turn back the tips. If I don't, a pipe cleaner will eventually poke through the end of the finger. Not a pretty sight.

21 Bend a pipe cleaner in half and insert one end into a finger and the other end in the next finger. Do the same with another pipe cleaner. You'll want the pipe cleaners in consecutive order—next to each other (figure h).

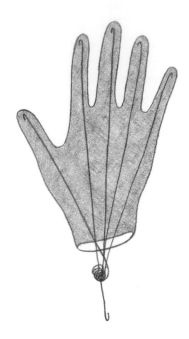

(figure h)
Wire the fingers.

22 Keep one pipe cleaner straight and insert it into the thumb. Just past the wrist, wrap the straight pipe cleaner around the other two. This secures the pipe cleaners, keeping them in place. Repeat for other hand.

Tip:
- - - - - - - - - - - - - - -

As you wrap the straight pipe cleaner around the others, hold the others firmly with your hand. Wrapping the ends prevents the opposite ends from coming out of the fingers.

23 Fill just the palm side of each hand with stuffing. You will need to decide which hand is the left and which is the right before you do this. As you fill the palms with stuffing you'll notice that this pushes the pipe cleaners against the back of the hand. This gives the effect of bones.

24 To sculpt the hand, thread a needle with ¾ yard (0.69 m) strong thread. Place a knot in the single end. Attach this to the inside of the hand, in the seam below the thumb. Push the needle to the outside just in from the thumb, at the wrist. Take the needle and thread across the wrist and into the wrist just short of the seam under the little finger. Come out at the center of the palm.

25 Take the needle across the palm toward the thumb and index finger and push the needle in just short of the seam. Come out just above the thread at the wrist (figure i). Couch the thread by making a small stitch that takes the needle across the wrist thread and into the wrist. Insert the needle through the wrist and then come out at the back of the hand, straight back from the stitch in the wrist. Push the needle back into the hand and come out at the palm. Take a small stitch and push the needle into the palm and down to the wrist.

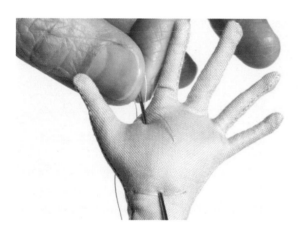

(figure i)
Sculpt the palm of the hand.

26 Take a small stitch where the needle just emerged, then push the needle back into the hand and out at the center of the palm, next to the beginning of the long diagonal stitch made in step 25. Push the needle into the hand, a small stitch this time, and come out at the back of the hand between the index and middle finger.

27 Taking vertical stitches, push the needle into the hand, under the pipe cleaner, and out between the middle and ring fingers (figure j). Push the needle back into the hand, under the pipe cleaner, and out between the ring and little finger.

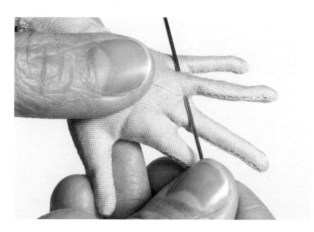

(figure j)
Sculpt the back of the hand.

28 After the hands are sculpted, hand sew them to the arms.

29 If your doll will have ears, such as Viviana in chapter 2, cut, sew, and attach them now (see Ears, page 34).

Tip:
- - - - - - - - - - - - - -

Stitching the hand in the recent steps sculpted the lifeline on the palm and lifted the knuckles on the back of the hand.

THE FACE GRID

1 Follow the illustration as you go through the various steps to draw the marks and lines with a mechanical pencil (figure k). The lengthwise seam on the face designates the center of the grid. To find the halfway point across the width, find the curve of the nose where it starts to shift out from the face, below the forehead. This is generally at the halfway point between the forehead and the chin. Place a pencil mark here, on either side of the center seam (#1).

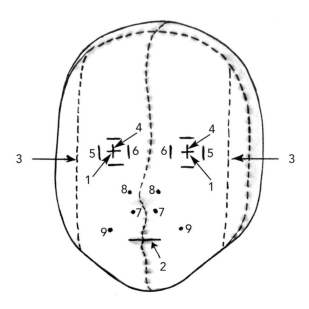

(figure k)
Draw a grid for the face.

2 Below the bottom curve of the nose, find the halfway point between the nose and the chin. This is the center of the mouth. Place a mark here (#2).

3 To locate the center of the eyes, it helps to locate the temple area and draw some dashed lines down each side of the face (#3).

4 Find the halfway point between one of these dashes and the center seam. Place a vertical pencil mark here (#4); it should fall on horizontal pencil mark #1. Make the same mark on the other side of the face.

5 From the slice between #3 and #4, find the halfway point. Make a vertical pencil mark here (#5). Make a mark the same length on the other side of the face.

6 Halfway between #4 and the center seam of the face, make a pencil mark (#6). You now have one eye width between the marks for the inner corners of each eye. The distance between #5 and #6 is the width of an eye.

7 Measure the width of one eye. The height of an eye is the same as the width. Make a pencil mark above and below #1 for the eye height. Draw a square using the pencil marks as references. An eyeball will fit inside each square.

8 The nostrils are next. Find a slight inward curve on the face. On either side of the center seam and directly down from #6 (the inside corner of the eye), make a small dot with the pencil (#7). Do the same on the other side of the face.

9 The flare of the nose is straight up from the nostrils and halfway to the lower inside corner of the eye. Make a pencil mark on both sides of the center seam (#8).

10 The outside corners of the lips are in a direct line with #4. Make a small dot with the pencil (#9) on both sides of the face and in line with the center of the mouth (#2).

THE FEATURES

1 Using a mechanical pencil, draw a large circle inside the square eye socket, for the eyeball. Draw a medium-sized circle inside the first one, for the iris. Place a smaller circle in the center of the second one, for the pupil (figure l). (Note: The largest circle has been covered with the eyelids in figure l.)

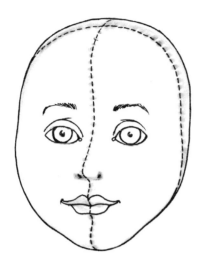

(figure l)
Draw a series of circles to make the features.

2 Draw the upper and lower eyelids next.

3 The eyebrows are slightly above the square you drew earlier for the eye socket, above points #5 and #6 on the face grid (figure k). The inside of the eyebrow starts straight up from the inside of the eye, arches above the outer edge of the eyeball and ends just slightly out from the outer edge of the eyeball. (Note: The nose will be sculpted so you needn't worry about it for now.)

4 The lips are a series of circles. Make a small one on the center seam for the turbuncle (or milkbud, the tiny circle in the center of the upper lip). On either side of this, draw larger circles, keeping them under the nose. Make the lower lip more of an oval shape.

5 Following the outer edges of the circles, outline the upper lip and lower lip and draw in the center of the lips.

6 With a brown fabric pen, outline the eyelids, iris, pupil, and lips. Erase all pencil marks except for the nostrils and nostril flares.

THE FACE SCULPTING

1 Thread the 3" (7.6 cm) -long sculpting needle with 1 yard (0.91 m) of strong thread. Knot one end. Anchor the thread by taking a stitch in the back of the head, behind the top seam. Hair will cover the knot. (Note: Without this small stitch, the knot might pop through the head and come out the front of the face.) Refer to the chart of sculpting points (figure m) as you work through the following steps.

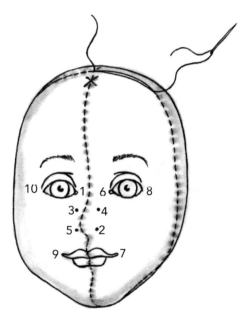

(figure m)
Shape the face following this Sculpting Points Chart.

2 Push the needle into the head and out at the inside corner of the eye (#1).

3 Go back into the head, but not too close to the place where you previously came out, with a vertical or horizontal stitch. Pull the needle and thread out at the opposite nostril (#2). From this point on, as you go in and out, start pulling on the thread to define the features. Keep the thread taut, but do not pull it too tightly. Shift the stuffing back into the nose while stitching. As you go in and out, dig down with your needle and catch quite a bit of stuffing between the needle and the surface of the head.

4 Insert the needle back into the head and pull it out the opposite side of the nose, at the flare (#3). Go back into the head and straight across to the other flare (#4).

5 Insert the needle into the head, down to the opposite nostril (#5), back into the head, and up to the opposite inside corner of the eye that was not stitched earlier (#6).

6 Working on the same side of the face throughout this step, insert the needle back into the head and down to the outside corner of the mouth (#7). Go back into the head and up to the outside corner of the eye (#8).

7 Insert the needle and thread back into the head and pull out at the inside corner of opposite eye (#1). Working on the same side of the face for the rest of this step, go back into the head and down to the outside corner of the lips (#9). Pull out here and then go back inside the head and up to the outside corner of the eye (#10). Insert the needle back into the head, then pull the thread through to the back of the head and anchor it off by taking a couple of small stitches.

COLORING THE HEAD

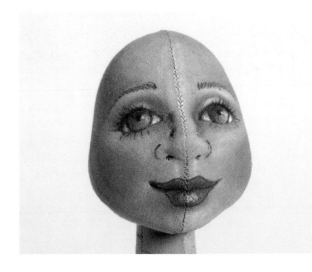

(figure n)
Colors blend together beautifully on this sample head.

1 With sienna brown, scribble down the temples, around the crease of the upper eyelid (even though it isn't there yet), down both sides of the nose, under the nose, around the nose flares, down the center seam under the tip of the nose, under the lower lip, and around the chin area (figure n).

2 On the side that will have shadows, shade in a bit beyond the chin, toward the cheek. Shade lightly on the upper lip, around the crease of the smile, and under the lower eyelids (figure o).

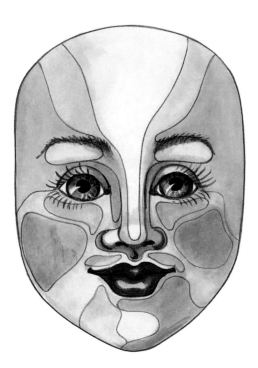

(figure o)
Shade the face to imply dimension by following this color chart.

3 With a lighter tan, beige, or flesh-colored pencil, bring the highlights into the face, next to the darker brown and heading toward the higher points. Place the highlights next to the temples, down the sides of the nose, the upper lip, the chin, on the cheekbones under the eyes, and on the brow bone just below the eyebrows.

4 With a white pencil, lighten the center of the forehead, the cheekbones under the eyes, and the center of the chin. Place the white directly on top—and in the center—of the highlights. The white may not be visible on your fabric but it is very important.

5 With the carmine red, blush the cheek.

6 Wrap a piece of fabric around your index finger and blend all of the colors together.

7 The doll's eyes are varying shades of one color or three colors. You will need a light, medium, and dark.

8 With the lightest color, fill in the entire iris. On the side of the iris that would be in a shadow, use the middle color. Also apply the middle color underneath the upper eyelid. The darkest color starts on the inner edge of the upper eyelid and follows the eyelid over to the outer edge. The lower part of the eyelids catches the color from the eyes. Darken the upper part of the iris with this color, touching the upper part of the pupil.

9 Fill in both the upper and lower lip with a lighter red. Darken the upper lip and the lower part of the lower lip with a darker red.

10 Using a white pencil, lighten the center of the lower lip.

11 Seal the face with a textile medium and let the face dry for twenty-four hours.

12 Using a brown pen, outline the eyelids, draw in the eyelashes, and feather in the eyebrows.

13 With the brown pen, apply a dot for each nostril and then draw half circles on either side of the nose to represent the flares.

14 Outline the lips with a red pen.

15 With a contrasting color of pen, outline the irises and draw in the rods that radiate out from the pupil.

16 Color the pupil with a black pen.

17 Add a dot of white with the white gel pen in the pupil.

18 Seal the face again.

ATTACHING THE HEAD TO THE NECK

1 Grab the neck with a pair of hemostats and pinch it closed.

2 Rock the head on to the pinched neck, then ladder stitch the head to neck. The body is now ready to be clothed and beaded in the next chapter.

3 Sew hair to the head, following the instructions on page 47. (Note: Do not attach the hair if you are making Franalizia of the North Sea, which is in chapter 5.)

Beading supplies

BEADING BASICS

Because this book is about beading, there are a few essential things that you should know: the different types of beads and tools to make your life easier, and especially, how to get a bead needle threaded.

Many of you will notice that all size 11 seed beads aren't always the same size. This has a lot to do with the manufacturing companies. You'll find that seed beads made in Japan are more uniform. But, again, this varies from one manufacturer to the next. Toho Co. Ltd. and Miyuki Company are my preferred Japanese seed bead companies because both of these companies create even-sized seed beads. You will find that a Toho Treasure size 12 seed bead will be a little different in size compared to Miyuki. That means it's best to stick with one company, if you can.

Delica beads are also made in Japan, by Miyuki. Delicas are perfectly cut so that they fit flat next to each other. Whenever you see a definite design or pattern, such as a beaded pouch, it was made using Delicas. Toho makes a similar bead called an Aiko. Some find that the Aikos are nearly perfect in their uniformity.

Companies in the Czech Republic also make seed beads. Products from this country have smaller holes and aren't cut as precisely as the Japanese seed beads.

Another bead that is called for in the following chapters is a charlotte. This type of bead is cut on one side to give a sparkle effect. Some people consider these the most brilliant seed beads.

Crystals come in all sizes and shapes. Swarovski is the main manufacturer of crystals. There are other companies that make crystals, but they aren't as beautiful as the Swarovski crystals, which are made in the Czech Republic.

Miracle beads are so called because each one appears to have another bead inside it. Actually, the illusion is created by spraying the bead several times with a reflective material and then finishing it with a clear coating. Miracle beads are plastic and made in Japan.

Other types of beads are lampwork (glass), flower and leaf shapes, heat-set crystals (called Hot-Fix by Swarovski), wood, bone, ethnic, and semiprecious. If there is a bead not mentioned here, its use will be explained in the following chapters.

The size beading thread should coincide with the size bead you are working with. For instance, for bead sizes 10 and 11, a size B thread is generally used. For smaller beads, such as size 15, use 00 or 0 size thread. If you're using Japanese seed beads, you can use a B thread for the smaller seed beads. But with Czech beads, you'll need the thinner thread.

The same rule applies to beading needles. The smaller the bead, the smaller the eye of the needle. I find that a size 12 beading needle works with nearly all seed beads, except some Czech beads. Those beads with really small holes I throw away.

Thread conditioners come in several types. Beeswax is preferred by some and others like Thread Heaven, a nontoxic, acid-free conditioner that doesn't deteriorate over time. Beeswax and Thread Heaven prevent the thread from tangling and knotting.

To help keep your beads in place as you work, a piece of Ultrasuede or real suede is very helpful. You can pour the beads onto this surface so that the needle will pick up the beads easily. Or, you can place your working trays onto this surface and they'll stay in place, rather than scooting around.

Ever since the first iron needle with an eye was invented in the fifteenth century, we have had our ups and downs (or ins and outs) trying to thread the evasive small needle. Here's how I've managed to do it—no sure-fire guarantee, but close.

Use very sharp scissors and cut the thread straight across the end. Pinch the cut end between your index finger and thumb. You'll want just a small amount showing. With the needle in your other hand, lay the eye of the needle down on the thread. The thread should go into the eye easily. If it doesn't, lick the eye of the needle and try again. Licking the end of the needle seems to help the thread jump through the eye. I remember my grandmothers doing this and am happy to pass along what I learned from these wonderful ladies to you.

Now that you've threaded your needle...and have your doll in hand, the following chapters will help you put it all together with details on beading techniques and how to use the needles and threads.

Terms

Needle Over: Weave a threaded needle through one or two beads (as specified) and come out another bead.

Needling/Needle Up/Needle Through: Pull a threaded needle through one or more beads.

Picot: Several beads (usually three) joined by a length of thread that starts and ends in the same position.

Stack: Several beads sitting together, so that one is on top of the next. A short stack is a few beads that sit on the bead or fabric surface. A long stack is fringe. The uppermost bead in a stack is a stop bead.

Step Up: Used mainly in circular peyote stitch. At the end of a row, needle through the first bead in the same row and then add a bead to start the next row.

Stop Bead: Used in two different ways, the function remains the same: to stop other beads from falling off a length of thread. When planning to needle several beads onto a new, loose thread, start by placing only the first bead on the thread, leaving a tail beyond the end of the bead. Use a square knot (page 29) to tie this tail to the opposite, working thread length. Again, pull the needle and thread through the first bead. You have created a stop bead. Additional beads can now be needled as desired, and they will not fall off as you bead. A stop bead can also be a small bead added at the top of a bead stack, so that the ones underneath are snug against one another. For beginner beaders, a stop bead will alleviate the frustration of beads falling off the thread.

Up Bead: Protrudes up or down beyond the current row or the beaded surface. This is commonly found in peyote beadwork, but is not limited to this type of stitching.

BEADING AND EMBROIDERY TECHNIQUES

Adding Thread to Beadwork and Making a Loop Knot (Double Half Hitch)

1   When it is time to end thread, weave the needle and working thread through three beads (figure p). Come out between beads #3 and #4 and make a loop knot with the working needle and thread.

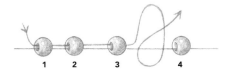

(figure p)
Right: Loop knot
Make a loop knot to start or end thread.

2   To make a loop knot, take the needle under the thread between the two beads; as you pull the thread you will see a loop being created. Push the needle into the middle of the loop and pull tight to create a knot. Do this twice more. Cut the thread.

3   To add thread, after threading the needle, weave through three beads and then make a loop knot.

Backstitch

1 Anchor the thread on the wrong side of the fabric or beadwork. Push the needle through the fabric, coming out on the right side. Needle up seven beads (figure q). Lay this flat against the surface of the fabric. Push the needle into the fabric, coming out on the wrong side.

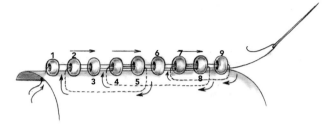

(figure q)
Backstitch
Work beaded backstitching like embroidery backstitching.

2 Move the needle over toward the middle of the row. Push the needle into the fabric and come out between beads #3 and #4.

3 Needle through beads #4 and #5, and then push the needle in to the fabric between #5 and #6. Come back up through the fabric and into #7. Come out #7 and add seven more beads.

4 Continue adding beads, filling in as you please.

Blanket Stitch

This form of blanket stitch is used to cover washers. It is similar to the embroidery stitch, but starts out differently due to the surface it is covering.

1 Cut 2 yards (1.83 m) of an embroidery-like thread. This can be Kreinik ribbon thread or YLI Candlelight thread. Thread a tapestry, or other large-eye, needle with this thread.

2 Tie the thread around the washer, leaving a short tail. Starting from the front, bring the needle into the opening of the washer, under the washer, and then over the thread (figure r). Pull tightly. Continue creating this stitch until the washer is completely covered. Weave the end of the thread through the stitches and cut. Cut the tail too.

(figure r)
Leave the thread crossover at the outer edge for the blanket stitch.

Flat Even-Count Peyote Stitch

1 Begin by needling up an even number of beads; in this example eight are used (figure s). This completes the base. (Notes: In *Creative Cloth Doll Beading*, the first line of beads does not count as a row. Each line of the illustration is shown in a different color. Line colors do not represent a change in actual bead color.)

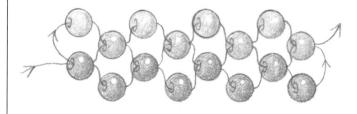

(figure s)
Flat peyote stitch
Skip beads in previous row to create peyote stitch beading.

Rows colored for identification only

2 Turn the needle around, pointing toward the thread tail. Add a new bead (#9), skip the last bead in the base row (#8) and go through bead #7. Add a new bead (#10), skip #6 and go through #5. Continue adding beads in the same manner until you have needled through #1. This completes the first row.

3 Turn the needle around, pointing toward the finished (opposite) end. Add a new bead (#13), skip #1, and go through #12 (an up bead). Add a bead, skip a bead, and go through a bead along the work (as you did in step 2). This completes the second row. Continue adding rows until you have worked the number desired.

Ladder Stitch

1 Stitch down from the front of the piece (#1) (figure t).

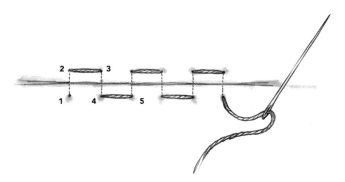

(figure t)
Ladder stitch
Use ladder stitching to join fabric pieces.

2 Hiding the thread, go into and out at the seam (#2).

3 Run the needle under the fabric for a bit and then take the needle out through the fabric (#3).

4 Push the needle into the fabric at #4.

5 Run the needle under the fabric for a bit and take the needle out through the fabric at #5.

6 Continue this process until the seam is finished.

Picot Edging

1 Anchor the thread at the back of the fabric or beadwork. Add three size 11 seed beads and push the needle into the fabric next to the spot you came out. This creates the first picot.

2 Take a small stitch in the back of the fabric and come through the last bead added, bead #3. Add two new size 11 seed beads and push the needle into the fabric next to bead #3 (figure u). Continue adding two beads as you continue along the edge of your piece.

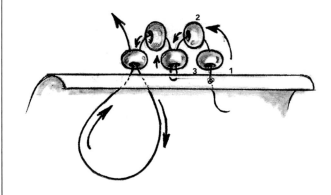

(figure u)
Picot edging
Add two beads for each new picot.

Simple or Basic Fringe

1 Anchor the thread on the wrong side of the fabric or beadwork. Push the needle through the fabric or out a bead.

2 Needle up an odd number of size 11 beads. At the end, add an accent bead and then a size 15 bead (for a picot) or a stop bead (figure v). Skip the size 15 beads or stop bead and needle through the rest of the beads.

(figure v)
Simple fringe
On fabric or beaded surface, stack beads
to make fringe.

Square Knot

1 Form a loop with the left thread. Bring the right thread through the loop from bottom to top, then underneath the entire left loop.

2 Now bring the right thread through the loop from top to bottom (figure w).

(figure w)
Weave yarn ends to create a square knot.

Chapter 2

Flowers
All
Around

Viviana

Visions of Viviana. The inspiration for this doll was flowers, all kinds of delightful flowers: flowers in her hair, in her basket, tattooed on her calves, and sparkling on her clothing. Each flower is a bit different. That's part of our bead-filled adventure. Some flowers are made from seed beads, others are created from fabric and then covered with beads, and others are built around washers found at the hardware store.

Viviana's bodice and skirt are embellished with seed beads. Her shoes and bouquet feature seed beads and washers. The featured flowers are in different forms, but the techniques are easy and can add a wide range of embellishment opportunities for your lovely doll.

Materials

- ✳ Basic Body (page 14) Note: Ears are made to create a more fairylike creature (see Ears, page 34)

- ✳ ½ yard (0.46 m) of 4½" (11.4 cm)-wide white or natural-colored lace for the upper skirt

- ✳ ½ yard (0.46 m) of 10½" (26.7 cm)-wide white or natural-colored lace for the underskirt

- ✳ 1 white or natural-colored lace motif for the bodice, about 12" (30.5 cm) long and wide enough to cover the doll as desired

- ✳ 1 lace motif for the underwear

- ✳ 12" (30.5 cm) square of fabric for both shoe soles

- ✳ 3 colors of polyester organza, each 5" x 11" (12.7 x 27.9 cm) for the wings

- ✳ 5½" (14 cm) fabric square for each beaded mum

- ✳ 2 squares, each 6" (15.2 cm), of soft fabric, such as velvet, rayon, or silky polyester for the basket

- ✳ machine-sewing thread color matched to the fabrics

- ✳ decorative sewing machine threads, thin enough to go through a sewing machine needle, for the wings and basket

- ✳ 2 pieces of water-soluble stabilizer, each 5" x 11" (12.7 x 27.9 cm) for the wings

- ✳ small pompom (optional) for each beaded mum

- ✳ 2 yards (1.8 m) of 26-gauge beading wire for the wings

- ✳ mohair for the hair

- ✳ 1 pipe cleaner for the ears

- ✳ 3" x 6" (7.6 x 15.2 cm) noncorrugated card-board for both Shoe Sole Inserts

- ✳ craft foam such as Softsculpt for the basket

Tools

- ✳ basic clothing, sewing, and beading kits (pages 12 and 13)

- ✳ tea strainer or other small shape for the basket

- ✳ soldering iron with fine point for the wings

- ✳ ballpoint pen

Bead Supplies

- ✳ size 11/12 seed beads in five colors: 20 grams of each for the upper skirt, bodice, shoes, small five-point flowers, six-point flowers, beaded cuff, Haku Lei, marguerite flowers, wings (optional), and basket (Note: 1 color should be green for the leaves)

- ✳ size 14/15 seed beads in five colors: 20 grams of each color for the washer flowers, beaded mums, tattoos, and wings (optional)

- ✳ 3 mm and 4 mm bicone crystals in three colors: seven of each color and each size (forty-two total) for the washer flowers (4 mm only), six-point flower, wings (optional), and tattoos

- ✳ 6 mm marguerites: three for the marguerite flower, wings (optional), and cuff

- ✳ 5 mm drop beads in several colors: approximately twenty of each for the upper skirt, wings (optional), and sleeves

- ✳ size 15/0 gold and silver charlottes: 10 grams total for the upper skirt, marguerite flowers, beaded mums, wings (optional), and cuff

- ✳ 6 mm miracle beads: five for the wings (optional), one for each six-point flower, and one for each Haku Lei bud

- ✳ 3 mm heat-set crystals, such as Swarovski Hot-Fix, in various colors: fifty total for the clothing, wings (optional), and tattoos

- ✳ size B Nymo beading thread

- ✳ Twenty size 10 washers (as found in any hardware store) for the washer flowers

- ✳ metallic threads, such as Kreinik's fine braids and YLI's Candlelight, for the washer flowers

Paint Supplies

- ✳ inks that are permanent on metal, such as Tsukineko StazOn and Jacquard Pinata Color, for the washer flowers

- ✳ Jacquard Dye Na Flow in various colors to dye all of the lace

- ✳ Jacquard Lumiere metallic and pearlescent paints for the wings

- ✳ small and medium paint brushes for the washer flowers and wings

- ✳ unmounted rubber stamp in design of choice for the arm and leg tattoos

- ✳ stamp pad with ink formulated for fabric, such as Jacquard Pearl EX Stamp Pad or Tsukineko's Fabrico for the arm and leg tattoos

EARS

1 Trace two ears from the pattern (page 116) on the wrong side of the fabric used for the body. Double the fabric, right sides together, so that you can see both of the traced ears. Machine sew from the opening all the way around to the other side of the opening of both tracings. Cut out both ears, using scant ⅛" (3 mm) seam allowances, and clip the curves.

2 Using hemostats, turn the ears right side out. Trace the ear stitching lines on the pattern piece onto each ear, making sure you have a right and left ear. Machine sew the stitching line on each ear with matching thread, allowing room between the stitching line and the edge of the ear along the inner edge for the pipe cleaner to be inserted. Cut the threads.

3 Bend back the tip of one end of the pipe cleaner. Insert the pipe cleaner into the ear, in the "casing" along the outer edge of the ear until the tip is in the top of the ear (figure a). Cut the other end of the pipe cleaner about ¼" (6 mm) from the opening of the outer edge of the ear. Bend back this tip and push the rest of that end into the earlobe. Insert a small amount of stuffing in the inner edge of the ear. Close up the opening and hand stitch the ear to the side of the head, where marked on the pattern piece, using the ladder stitch (page 28).

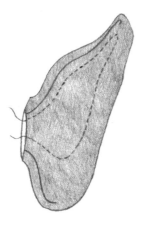

(figure a)
Topstitch ears and insert pipe cleaners.

ARM AND LEG BEAD TATTOOS

1 With the arms and legs still separate from the doll body, select a rubber stamp that is unmounted and has a design that you like. Ink this with the stamp pad and then apply it to the arm (figure b, below). Carefully wrap the rubber stamp around the arm and press with your fingers. Remove the rubber stamp by lifting straight up. It is not necessary to heat-set this stamp, as the design will be covered with beads. The sample doll (page 32) was stamped with Jacquard Pearl Ex Stamp Pad in Gold Violet.

(figure b)
Roll an unmounted stamp over the fabric.

2 Collect three or four colors of size 15 seed beads, two washer flowers (page 40), straight pins, beading needle, and beading thread. At the center of the design, using the beading needle and thread, hand sew the washer flower to the arm or leg. Depending on the amount of thread you have left, start bead embroidering over the stamped design. Use the backstitch (page 27) to anchor the beads to the design.

3 If the design you have chosen has points, as the sample doll has, fuse some heat-set crystals at the ends of the points. The sample doll's design has some curves. In order to follow the curves, place some straight pins along the design. Thread enough beads to follow the pins, then sight along them to help align and anchor the beads using the backstitch (figure c).

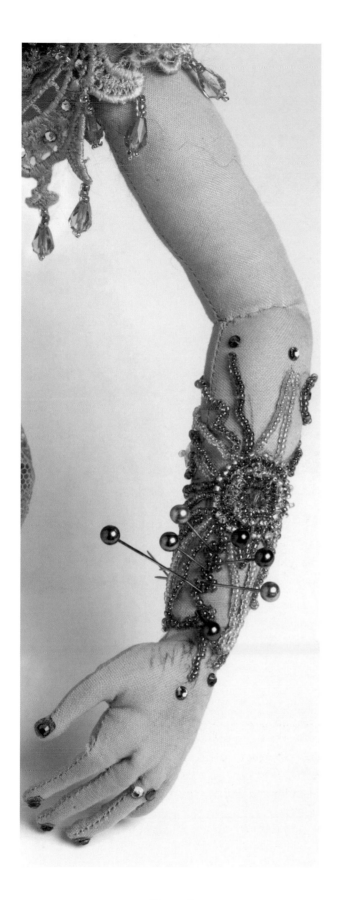

(figure c)
Sight along straight pins to align beads.

4 At the end of some of the shorter points of the design, add a 3 mm bicone crystal by pushing the needle into the arm or leg and coming out at the end of the stamped design. Place a bicone crystal and a size 15 seed bead on the needle. Take the beads to the arm or leg and hold them in place. Skipping the size 15 seed bead, push the needle into the crystal and into the arm. Continue adding the size 15 seed beads to the design.

BEADING CLOTHING AND SHOES

1 Decide on your color theme and pour the Dye Na Flow into containers.

2 Dip the lace for the underskirt into the dye. Remove it from the dye and squeeze out the excess dye. Hang it to dry.

Tip:

I like using an ice cube tray to hold the paint colors. This gives me several mixing containers, plus one for plain water. I color-dip larger pieces of lace because it is faster and easier than hand painting.

3 The rest of the lace is dyed using paintbrushes. Brush on the colors you want, allowing colors to bleed into each other. This creates a third color (figure d). The sample doll was made with Magenta and Periwinkle, with White added along with 30 percent water, creating the pastel colors. When all of the lace is dry, iron to set the colors.

(figure d)
Close-up of the dress

4 Machine sew the short ends of the upper skirt lace, right sides together, to make the back seam on the upper skirt. Before placing the skirt on the doll's body, add some of the heat-set crystals along the lower part of the lace. Next, hand sew some drop beads at various points on the lace. To do this, thread a beading needle with 1 yard (0.91 m) of beading thread. Place a knot in

the single end. Attach this to the back side of the lace, behind the spot where you will add a drop bead. Come through to the front of the lace. At each position, add three size 11 seed beads, a drop bead, and three size 15 gold or silver charlottes. Skip the three charlottes, insert the needle and thread back through the drop bead, three size 11 seed beads, and the lace (figure e). Anchor the thread at the back of the lace and cut the thread. Continue doing this along various points of the lace.

(figure e)
Add the drop beads to the lace.

5 For the underwear, pin the lace motif to the body. Hand sew it in place, trimming as necessary.

6 Machine sew the short ends of the underskirt lace, right sides together, to make the back seam on the underskirt. Separately machine sew a gathering running stitch along the waist (upper edge) of both the upper skirt and the underskirt. Pull the threads to loosely gather the edge, then slip it onto the doll and pull tightly. Slip the upper skirt on first, then the underskirt. Adjust the gathers, then hand sew the skirts to the body.

7 Pin the lace motif to the bust, back, and arms of the doll's body. Hand sew it in place. Add a scattering of size 11 seed beads as you hand sew the lace to the body. As with the skirt, add some drop beads to various points along the sleeves (figure f).

(figure f)
Close-up of sleeves

8 Trace two of the Shoe Sole pattern piece (page 116) onto the wrong side of a cotton fabric of choice. Cut a slit down the center of the drawn soles. Double the fabric, right sides together, and pin it in several places. Machine sew all the way around the traced lines, through both fabric layers. Cut out the shapes using a scant ⅛" (3 mm) seam allowance (figure g). Turn the sole right side out through this opening.

(figure g)
Cut slits through one layer of each seamed set.

9 Cut out two Shoe Sole Inserts (page 116) from cardboard. Slip these inside the soles, through the slits. Hand sew to close up the slits.

10 Collect the size 11 seed beads you want for the shoes. The shoes are made with one color for the shoe top and back, then different color beads for the ruffles and other embellishments. Using backstitch beadwork (page 27), anchor the thread at the back of the heel of the sole and lay down the beads by backstitching along the outer edge of the entire sole.

Tip:

I find it helpful to make a template of the sole. As I draw on to the fabric, I flip over the template for one of the soles. This way, I have a right and a left sole for the shoes. I then cut a slit down the center of the drawn side of each sole. This ensures that I do not cut through both layers when cutting the slit after the shoe is sewn.

11 With the same seed beads, do one row of peyote beadwork (page 27) on each sole, placing the new beads on top of the row applied in step 10. Do not cut the beading thread. Place the sole on to the doll's foot and decide where you want to do the beading to make the shoe back. Using a pencil, mark the placement of the shoe back. Needle over (page 26) to this spot and start adding rows of peyote beading—attached to, and built up from the shoe sole—back and forth, to create the heel. To angle the edges of the shoe back as shown on the sample doll (page 32), as you come to the end of a row, instead of adding a bead, turn the needle and go into the last bead of the current row. Add a bead (this will be the first bead of the next row), skip the next bead, and go through the third bead from the end of the row just worked (figure h). Continue across in peyote as usual. To create an angle at the end of the row, instead of adding a bead, turn the needle and go into the last bead of the previous row, then through the last bead of the current row. Add a bead (this will be the first bead of the next row), and go through the next (second) bead of the row just worked. (Note: Each row of the illustration is shown in a different color. Row colors do not represent a change in actual bead color.)

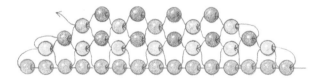

(figure h)
Angle row ends for shoe heel.
Rows colored for identification only

12 After the shoe back is finished, add two rows of ruffled edging to the shoe as follows: Thread the beading needle with 1½ yards (1.37 m) of beading thread. Place a knot in the single end and anchor it in the fabric in the sole of the shoe, at one side of the shoe back. Push the needle into an up bead at the beginning edge of the shoe back. Come out this bead and add three size 11 seed beads that are a different color from the shoe beads. Take the needle over to the next up bead and go into this bead. You have made a picot (ruffle). Come out

that bead and add another three beads of the same color as the previous picot. Continue doing this along the edge to the opposite side of the shoe back. Change to another bead color and do another row of picots next to the row you just finished. This gives a ruffled effect. Do not cut the thread yet.

13 Slip the shoe on the doll's foot and pin it in place. At this point, anchor the thread you have been working with into the foot of the doll. Anchor the shoe back to the foot in several places, then cut the thread close to the beadwork. Place another 2 yards (1.83 m) of beading thread on the needle and knot the end. Anchor this in the sole, near the place where the instep of the shoe would be. Thread up enough seed beads to go from one side of the shoe to the other side, over the top of the foot. Do not anchor this row to the foot. That is done later.

14 Using peyote beadwork, fill in the shoe top. Do not decrease at the edges (as done on the heel). When you get close to the toe, anchor the shoe top to the foot. To do this, push the needle from a bead into the foot. Move the needle over and come up in between two beads. Go through a couple of beads, then push the needle into the foot. Doing this three or four times anchors the shoe top firmly to the foot (figure i).

(figure i)
Close-up of the shoes

15 As with the shoe back, create picots, with two different colors of size 11 seed beads, along the toe edge and the top edge of the shoe top. Hand sew one of the beaded washer flowers (page 40) to the center of the shoe top

FLOWERS

Small Five-Point Flower

Viviana has five of these flowers attached at each shoulder. One flower is at the center of her bodice and fourteen are attached around the upper edge of her skirt, at the waist.

1 Thread a beading needle with 1 yard (0.91 m) of beading thread. Wax the thread.

2 Needle up five size 11 seed beads in one color. Tie these in a circle. Add one bead and then go into the next bead in the circle (figure j). (Note: Each round of the illustration is shown in a different color. Round colors do not represent a change in actual bead color.) Add another bead and go into the next bead in the circle. Continue this all the way around. Five new beads have been added. Carefully cut away the tail thread at the knot in the circle. Do not cut the working thread.

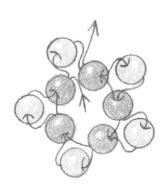

(figure j)
Tie beads in a circle and add five new beads.

Rounds colored for identification only

3 At the end of the most recent row, go through the first bead you added. This is an up bead. You will see four more up beads, which you just added in step 2. In this new row, add a bead and then go through an up bead. Repeat this four more times (figure k). (Note: Each round of the illustration is shown in a different color. Round colors do not represent a change in actual bead color.) Five new beads have been added. Go through the first bead you added in this round. Continue going around the circle, adding three more rounds in the same way. As you add these next rounds, start pulling on the threads so that your beads turn in to a cup.

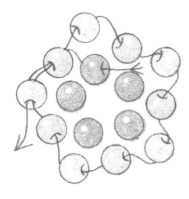

(figure k)
Add another (third) row of beads.

Rounds colored for identification only

4 Change the bead color and thread three size 11 seed beads of this second color. Take the needle into the next up bead of the previous round. Add three of the new color and go into the next up bead. Continue this process all the way around. When you come to the end, you will see that you have created a five-petal flower.

5 Weave the needle down through beads in the previous rows to the bottom, into one of the original five beads. Take the needle inside and up out the center of this bead. Add four of a third color of seed bead. This represents the stamen. Add one bead of another color. Skip this last bead and go back into the four seed beads, and then into the bottom center. Go through one of the original five beads, and then add another stamen. Create two more stamens.

6 After the stamens are made, leaves can be added along the outer edge, on the outside of the flower cup. Change to green seed beads. Going through the flower center from the inside to the outside, come out a bead of the original five. Add five green seed beads. Skip the last bead and go through just the fourth (second to last loaded) seed bead. Add three green seed beads and go over to another bead in the circle of original five beads (figure l). Create another leaf the same way. Leave enough thread to sew the flower to the doll or to the haku lei.

(figure l)
Add beaded leaves to the outside of the flower.

Rounds colored for identification only

7 After two leaves are made, attach the flower to the doll's waist or bodice.

Washer Flower

These flowers are at the center of the shoe tops and on her haku lei (head band).

1 Color a washer with ink from Tsukineko StazOn stamp pads.

2 Collect a painted washer, braids, ribbons, threads of choice, two colors of size 15 seed beads (colors A and B), a 4 mm bicone crystal for each flower, a beading needle, and FireLine beading thread. Cover the washer with

the threads by using the blanket stitch (page 27). Weave the thread and braid tails throughout the blanket stitch at the top. Fasten off the ends and cut off any extra threads.

3 Cut 2 yards (1.83 m) of FireLine and thread a beading needle. Place a knot in a single long end. Anchor this at the top of a blanket stitch on the washer. Place two color A, one color B, and two color A beads on the needle. Push the needle into the blanket stitch next to the one where you came out.

4 From the edge of the blanket stitch, go back into the last bead added and come out this bead. Add one color A, one color B, and two color A beads. Push the needle into the next blanket stitch (figure m). Continue making picots until you have gone all the way around the washer's top edge. When you get to the beads you started with, add one color A, one color B, and one color A. Go into the first bead of the first picot, and then into the first blanket stitch.

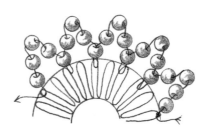

(figure m)
Edge washer with beaded ruffle.

5 If you have enough thread left, weave down through the blanket stitches to the center of the washer. Pick up a 4 mm crystal and go over to the other side and into the inner edge of the washer. Go back into the crystal and over to where you started. Do this two more times.

6 After the crystal is seated in the center of the washer, add another round of five-bead picots around the edge of the center (the inner edge of the washer) by working into the blanket stitches as you did on the outer edge. When this row is complete, go back into the threads covering the washer and tack down each of the center seed beads (color B). The goal is to get the top bead of each picot to lay flat against the blanket stitches. This keeps the beads from moving around and covering the crystal.

Marguerite Flower

Close-up of marguerite flowers

1 Collect a 6 mm crystal marguerite, size 15 gold or silver charlottes, size 11 seed beads in two colors for the flower (colors A and B) and one color for the leaves, a beading needle, and beading thread. Cut 2 yards (1.83 m) of beading thread and thread the needle with no knot in the end. Wax the thread.

2 Thread sixteen size 11 seed beads of color A. Tie a knot in the thread to form a circle. Work one round of peyote beading on the inside of the circle as follows: Add one bead of color A. Skip the first bead in the circle and then go through the next (second) bead. Add another color A bead. Skip the next bead in the circle and then go through the next bead in the circle. Continue doing this until you have eight beads in the

second round and you are back at the starting point (figure n, left). (Note: Each round of the illustration is shown in a different color. Round colors do not represent a change in actual bead color.)

3 The third round is also worked inside the circle, with color A seed beads. Go through the first bead in round two. Thread one seed bead and then go through the next two beads in round two. Add three more seed beads in the same way, so that the last round-two bead you go through is actually the first bead in round two—the same one you went through at the start of round three.

4 When you get to the first bead you added in the third round, go through that bead. With the same needle and thread, pick up the marguerite bead and a size 15 charlotte, either the gold or silver color. Skip the charlotte and pass through the marguerite, then over to the opposite side of round three, and into a round-three bead. Pass through this bead, then back into the marguerite, through the charlotte, back into the marguerite, and over to another round-three bead that you have not gone through before (figure n, right). This process anchors the marguerite in the center of the flower.

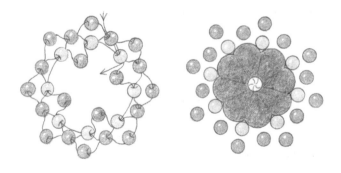

(figure n)
Work a base with peyote beading.
Rounds colored for identification only

5 As round two was worked, the round-one beads that were not used popped to the outside of the circle. These are up beads. Weave through the beads in the previous rounds, coming out an up bead along the outer edge. Thread three size 11 seed beads of color B and push the needle into the next up bead. Continue this all the way around the outer edge (figure o). (Note: Each round of the illustration is shown in a different color. Round colors do not represent a change in actual bead color.)

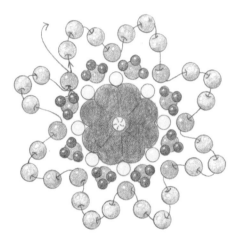

(figure o)
Add the center round.
Rounds colored for identification only

6 Now weave down to a center (round-two) bead in between the up beads and come out one of these. You are now working inside round two. Add three of the color B size 11 seed beads and go over to the next center, or down, bead and continue adding groups of three seed beads all the way around. After the picots are added, weave the needle to the back of the flower and add a beaded leaf or two (step 6 of the Small Five-Point Flower, page 39).

7 Attach the finished beaded flower to the doll skirt or haku lei (page 45). The sample doll has one marguerite flower at the center of the waist. Another marguerite flower was added to the haku lei.

Beaded Mum

1 Cut out three circles of fabric (or use the template on page 117). Thread a beading needle with beading thread and place a knot in the single end. Anchor this to the edge of one of the circles. Hand sew a gathering stitch along the edge. Roll a small amount of stuffing in your hands into a ball. Place this in the center of the fabric circle and pull the thread to close the fabric around the stuffing.

2 Collect size 15 seed beads in the colors you want for the mums. You will also need size 15 charlottes in colors of your choice. The sample doll has gold and silver charlottes at the end of each mum petal (see photo, page 32).

3 Push the needle into the edge of the round fabric ball and come out on the outside, at a spot close to the gathered edge. Thread five size 15 seed beads and then three size 15 charlottes. Skip the three charlottes and go into the last of the seed beads, just through the one bead. Come out this bead and add four seed beads. Push the needle into the ball next to where you added the beads. As you go into the fabric, adjust the three charlottes so that they form a picot at the top of the petal. Take the needle out of the ball, close to where you went in, and add another petal. Add three rounds of these petals, circling the perimeter of the ball.

4 For the rest of the mum, reduce the number of seed beads on each additional petal that you make: thread four size 15 seed beads and then three charlottes. Go into the last (fourth) seed bead and add three seed beads. Go into the fabric, then back out close to where you went in. Continue around the rest of the top of the ball until it is filled in.

Fabric circles, partially made beaded mum, and finished flower

Six-Point Flower

1 Collect two colors of size 11 seed beads and one accent bead for the center. This accent can be a miracle bead or a 4 mm bicone crystal. Thread a needle with 1 yard (0.91 m) of beading thread. Wax the thread. Thread twelve seed beads of one color. Tie the beads in a circle, leaving a 3" (7.6 cm) tail. Push the needle in to the first bead added and come out that one bead. Add five seed beads of the same color. Skip the next bead in the circle and go into the third bead (figure p, top). (Note: Each round of the illustration is shown in a different color. Round colors do not represent a change in actual bead color.) Come out that third bead and add five more seed beads. Continue around the circle in the same way. At the end of the round, you weave through the same bead that you did at the beginning. You will have six five-bead petals (picots).

2 Push the needle into the first two beads of the petal closest to where your needle just came out (these are round-two beads). Come out the second bead. Thread up five seed beads of the same color. Skip the third bead of the same five-bead petal made in round two and go into the fourth bead. Come out this bead and add one bead. Push the needle into the second bead of the next petal and come out that bead. Add five seed beads, skip the third bead of the same petal, and

go into the fourth bead. Come out that bead and add one bead. Continue in the same way all the way around the circle of petals (figure p, bottom). At the end, add one seed bead as usual and then push the needle into the second bead of the next petal, but now take the needle down to the center circle of beads (round one).

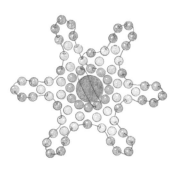

(figure p)
Add central accent bead last.
Rounds colored for identification only

3 Weave down to the bead between the first five-bead petal made in round two. Come out that bead. Following steps 1 and 2, add another row of petals, going from one center bead (between the original petal beads) to the next center bead.

4 Weave down into the center of the circle and pick up the accent bead. Take the needle and push it into a center bead across from the bead you came out. Come out this bead then back into the accent bead and into a bead near where you started. Attach this flower to the haku lei, or wherever you want.

BEADED CUFF

Close-up of beaded cuff

1 Collect the size 11 seed beads, marguerites, and charlottes you want for the cuff on Viviana's right arm. Cut 2 yards (1.83 m) of beading thread and thread the beading needle. Thread enough beads to wrap around Viviana's wrist. If necessary, place a stop bead (page 26) at the end of the thread, then add the seed beads.

2 Following the peyote beadwork instructions (page 27), create seven rows. Place this on the doll's wrist and weave the cuff closed. Push the needle through the top bead and then into the second bead on the opposite side. Come out that bead and go into the third bead on the side you started on. Come out that bead and go over to the fourth bead on the opposite side. Continue weaving down to the bottom, then back up to the top, in the same way (figure q). This closes the cuff around the doll's wrist.

(figure q)
Weave the ends together to make a circle.

3 Weave through the beads and come out along the top edge. Change colors of seed beads and add a three-bead picot along the edge. To do this, bring the needle out a bead, add three beads, then push the needle down into the next edge bead. Bring the needle out that bead. Add three beads and push the needle into the next edge bead. Continue all the way around the top edge this way.

4 Weave the needle down to the center of the cuff and bring the needle out a bead. Add one marguerite and three silver size 15 charlottes. Skipping the three charlottes, push the needle back into the marguerite then into the seed bead of the cuff. Weave the needle down to the bottom edge of the cuff and add a row of picots along this edge, as done on the top edge. Anchor the thread either in the arm or between the beads and then cut the thread.

HAKU LEI

While living in Hawaii, this was my favorite type of lei. Haku means "head" in Hawaiian, thus, head lei. It is beautiful and will add just the right finishing touch to the doll.

Close-up of haku lei

1 Make a variety of flowers following the instructions earlier in this chapter. Collect size 11 green seed beads, beading needle, and beading thread. Cut 2 yards (1.83 m) of beading thread and place it in the needle. Wax the thread. Thread enough beads to wrap around the doll's head, and then add another five beads. The lei should be a bit loose as adding the flowers, leaves, and buds will make it shrink a bit.

2 Tie these beads in a circle. Work peyote beading for two rounds around the circle, using the green seed beads. Pick up a flower and anchor it to the circle of beads as follows: Push the needle inside two beads at the lower center of the flower then into two beads on the circle. Anchor the flower in this way at least three more times. After the flower is anchored, add two or three beaded leaves as done in step 6 of the Small Five-Point Flower (page 39). Continue adding flowers and leaves until the lei is covered.

3 To create buds, push the needle into a green seed bead at the base of the haku lei. Come out that bead and thread a miracle bead and a size 11 seed bead. Skip the size 11 seed bead and push the needle into the miracle bead and the bead you came out of on the haku lei. Add as many of these buds as you want.

WINGS

1 Collect three different colors of polyester organza, water-soluble stabilizer, decorative machine threads that are thin enough to go through a sewing machine needle, wing template (page 116), and beading wire. Trace the wing design on to the water-soluble stabilizer using a ballpoint pen. Layer the three colors of organza and pin them together with the stabilizer on top. Pin in several places to hold all of the layers in place.

2 Place decorative threads in both the needle and bobbin of your sewing machine. Place a darning or free-motion foot on the machine. Lower or cover the feed dogs, if you can. Lower the stitch length on the machine to 0 (smallest possible satin stitch length). This slows down the feed dogs, which helps with the free-motion sewing if you cannot lower them.

3 Following the drawn lines, machine sew the design. Once the wings are filled in, remove the darning or free-motion foot and place a cording foot on your machine, if you have one. If not, use an embroidery or zigzag presser foot.

Tip:

A cording foot has a small hole in the center of the toe, which allows you to place threads or wires through it. As you zigzag along the item, the material feeding through the hole is controlled to prevent the needle from hitting the threads or wires. On a Bernina, this foot is #6.

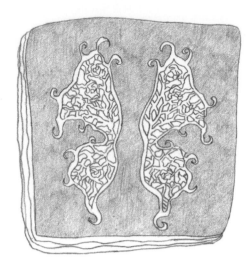

(figure r)
Layer organza and stabilizer
with traced wing template.

4 If you have a cording foot, push the wire through the small hole. Set the machine to zigzag and lower the stitch length to ½ (very short). Zigzag along the lines designated for the wire placement (figure r). It helps to not cut the wire from the spool until you have finished placing the section of the wire. Then cut the wire and insert it in the foot and zigzag the wire in place along the next area. Cut the wire, leaving 1" (2.5 cm) tail.

5 Cut closely and carefully around the design, making sure you do not cut through any of the stitches (figure s). Place the wings in a sink of lukewarm water to dissolve the stabilizer. After five minutes, remove the wings from the water and rinse them under running water. Pat them dry with a towel and hang them to dry.

6 When dry, plug in a soldering iron that has a fine tapered point. Once hot, carefully burn away parts of the design. The grayed areas of the template are the parts to be burned away. You may choose to burn away less or more. While the soldering iron is still hot, carefully seal the outer edges of the wings.

7 Once the wings are to your liking, turn on the heat-setting tool and add some heat-set crystals, if you want. You may also hand sew crystals or other beads to the

(figure s)
Stitch wings, add wire, then cut away excess stabilizer.

wings. There are a few scattered along Viviana's wings, arms, legs, and chest. A few were added to her face too.

8 Hand sew the wings to the back of Viviana's body near where her shoulder blades would be.

Tip:

When working with polyester and heating elements, always work in a well-ventilated area. A dust mask is recommended too. Because this product melts, watch your fingers. The burned-away fibers remain hot for about a minute. You might want to keep a small bowl of water handy to soothe hurt fingertips and a fire extinguisher nearby in case something catches fire.

ATTACHING THE HAIR

1 Hair is created last. Otherwise, it simply gets in the way. Collect the hair you have chosen for Viviana. You will also need a hand-sewing needle and strong thread, such as quilting thread. Cut 1 yard (0.91 m) of the thread and thread the needle with this. Place a knot in the single end.

2 Starting at the back of the head near the neck, hand sew a clump of the hair you have chosen. To make sure you have the clump secured, come out one side, at its center, and push the needle into the head next to where you came out, with the clump on the inside of the threads. Follow the seam line around the head, leaving ½" (1.3 cm) gaps between each clump. Add two or three clumps at the center of the head back. Fluff up the hair with your fingers and secure the style you want with a hand-sewing needle and strong hand-sewing thread.

3 Place the haku lei on Viviana's head and arrange. Pin it in place and then, with needle and thread, sew the lei to the head, catching the green base beads as you sew.

Use any brand of craft foam for the finished basket.

BASKET FOR FLOWERS

1 Collect the fabrics you want for the outside and lining of the basket and a tea strainer or other shape for the craft foam. Cut a circle shape from the craft foam (or use the template on page 117). Lay this on the fabrics you have chosen and cut them ⅓" (8 mm) larger. Sandwich the craft foam between the two fabrics with the right sides of both fabric pieces facing out.

2 Using decorative threads in your sewing machine needle and bobbin, randomly stitch all three pieces together. Do not position the stitches too close together, as you want room for the foam to shrink and form in to the shape you want.

3 Preheat your oven to 300°F (150°C). Place the shape in the oven and bake for only 60 seconds. Remove and immediately form over the shape you want. Viviana's basket was formed over a tea strainer. Hold in place for about 30 seconds. The craft foam will not be too hot to handle.

4 Using size 11 seed beads, add a picot edging (page 28) around the edge of the basket. Add accent beads here and there along the outer part of the basket. Make some beaded flowers by following the instructions earlier in this chapter. Hand sew some of them inside the basket, then fill with other beaded flowers, if you want.

Viviana is now ready to finish gathering her flowers and maybe make a neck lei for herself.

GALLERY

Jolie Fleur

JUDY BROWN

The artist writes:

On a recent vacation in the south of France, I was amazed by the beautiful colors of the flowers and countryside. This experience became my inspiration for my fairy. I named my doll Jolie Fleur, French for pretty flower.

Her bodice and hat are made of wool felt and her skirt of cotton netting and a floral silk. The wings were fashioned from organza and embroidered with metallic thread, then painted with Lumiere paints. I then attached Swarovski crystals to the edges of her wings. I wanted it to look as though she had a flower bud on the top of her head. I made a hat block with a stem out of aluminum foil and then stretched a wet square of wool felt over the foil form. At the bottom of the form, I gathered the fabric with a rubber band. I then used my steam iron to press the felt until all the gathers had fused together. After the rubber band was removed, I cut the bottom-ruffled edge into pointed petals. I beaded a vine, using size 14 seed beads to encircle the brim of her hat, and then attached eleven small five-pointed flowers. The focal point of her outfit is the beaded floral belt arrangement at her waist. I used peyote, brick, and herringbone stitch to make the flowers and leaves and then attached each component to the peyote belt in a pleasing arrangement. Her sandals are made of felt with leather soles and embellished with silk ribbon trim with a beaded rose at the center and tied with silk ribbons. Finally, she is wearing a Swarovski crystal around her neck, tied with hand-dyed silk ribbon from South Africa, the color of which is appropriately named "Fairies."

Rosella the Sprite of the Eastern Rosella

JENNY CAMPBELL

The artist writes:

The Australian bush was in bloom when I was thinking about what type of doll to do. Most of the iron bark eucalyptus trees were in flower and a creamy white haze adorned the skyline, the school yard, and the trees close to our house. Among the trees was my favorite bird: the Eastern Rosella. One morning while opening the back gate at school, I watched a mob of Rosella fly down and alight in front of me. They were a flurry of wings and color; there was my doll—a Rosella sprite alighting with her mob of birds. I made the fabric for the body, arms, and legs using a layer of rainbow organza covered in netting with all sorts of toning fabrics cut into small pieces between the layers. The machine embroidery over the sandwich of fabrics was completed with a rainbow-variegated cotton and feed dogs down. Hand-painted Tyvek became her jacket, wings, and shoes.

I love peyote, brick stitch, and threading, but I love the "Campbell" stitch best of all. Don't follow a pattern, simply thread and stitch and add beads wherever you want them; the hardest thing is trying to do the same thing twice. (Maybe that is why one follows a pattern.) I did complete a picot edge on her jacket and several leaf shapes for her hair. The white flowers in her hair represent the blossom on the iron barks, as do the flowers on her bag and at her throat. She has a twisted chain of green beads around her waist and many hanging threads of beads. Once Rosella's head was finished, it was attached and the last few hair feathers were stitched in place.

Fleur Labeade

KATHRYN HOWAT-FLINTOFF

The artist writes:

Since beading was the focus for this doll, I decided to use the body pattern #2 from *Creative Cloth Doll Making* (see Resources, page 121), as I wanted a larger canvas to work on. I wanted to do what I call "free-form" beading.

I took a literal approach to my assignment "flowers for her hair," beading stamens in to ready-made organza and satin flowers. The headdress behind represents the leaves. The odd butterfly landed on the flowers during the process.

I beaded at will (meaning that I picked up beads in no particular order) along and across her shoulders, to a V shape at the back of her neck. I then layered several complementary-colored fabrics on her abdomen and attached the leaf beads and a large peyote flower. The flower was made by first gluing a large glass bauble with the flat side to a piece of felt, and then I made a peyote flower following the instructions in *Creative Cloth Doll Faces* (see Resources, page 121). Her sandals and gloves are also made with free-form beading. As no self-respecting young woman would be seen out about town without a properly attired undercarriage, she is sporting a G-string made of machine-embroidered freestanding lace with a bead "string" securing it in place. As Fleur Labeade has traveled all the way from New Zealand, she could not resist wearing a paua necklace.

Strelitzia Fuoco

LORRAINE ABERNETHY

The artist writes:

Beading! How else to take this doll right over the top? I like to use materials in my work that aren't necessarily prescribed, for example, using nuts, bolts, and brass screws as if they were fine jewelry. I made my own beads for her hair using plastic drinking straws covered in fabric. I cut strips of fine silk and taffeta about 1" (2.5 cm) wide and the length of the straws on the straight grain of the fabric. I used watered-down PVA glue to saturate each fabric strip, then pressed it firmly with fingers onto the straws. I let the covered straws dry resting across the top of a bowl or jug. When dry, I cut to desired lengths and stitched these to the doll's head using four stitches at the base of the straw bead to secure. I painted the ends of the straws with acrylic paint to match. I wrapped some metallic thread around each bead, crisscrossing all over her head. I then cut 6" (15.2 cm) pieces of fringy yarn, folded in half twice, and using a fine pair of tweezers and PVA glue, I stuffed each bead with a tuft.

Using seed beads to make a netted trim for the ends of her sleeves, I finished the peaks with a large crystal in a contrasting color. I made a three-petal decoration with seed beads using peyote stitch for the front of her bust. I made a little beaded flower for her hair from the instructions in *Creative Cloth Doll Faces* (see Resources, page 121). I used very small seed beads that made the flower fold over on itself to create a nice contrast to the firm, rigid beads.

The feet were decorated with sequins and small beads in a random pattern. Look closely at her heart-shaped scepters; they are all beaded using a variety of beads, but one of them has brass eyelets stitched around the edge held in place by two beads.

Chapter 3

Embroidered Faces

The Mermaid

BY ANNE HESSE

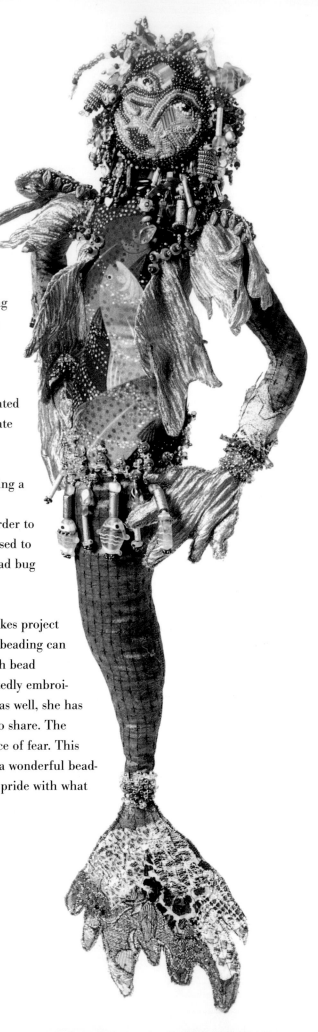

Anne Hesse has been beading for years, but learned bead embroidery more recently. On early weavings, fabric arts, and dolls, she used masses of large-holed beads, strung together on leather lacing as embellishments. She made lovely clay bead necklaces and bracelets by stringing her own handmade clay beads with other manufactured beads.

However, when she delved deeper in to doll making, she wanted to combine her own style of doll design with more appropriate beadwork. This meant going smaller.

She was intimidated by many of the instructional books. Being a visual learner, each time she read the "how to's," she would read more into them than there was, making them seem harder to follow. She went to her good friend, Gabe Cyr, who was pleased to show her the basics. From then on, she was smitten! The bead bug crawled into her system and has made itself at home.

Anne does not consider herself an expert beader. She still takes project classes, simply to keep learning and for the camaraderie, as beading can be isolating and is a solitary activity. But her experience with bead embroidery has given her a certain confidence. From repeatedly embroidering beaded faces for her own figures, and costume parts as well, she has learned some great techniques and has many valuable tips to share. The main thing she hopes you, the reader, bring to this is absence of fear. This chapter offers her clear and simple instructions for making a wonderful bead-embroidered face, so that you, too, will feel satisfaction and pride with what you create.

Materials

* 4" (10.2 cm) square of muslin or soft, light-colored cotton for the face
* 4" (10.2 cm) square of Pellon Stitch-n-Tear for stabilizing the face
* 4" x 8" (10.2 x 20.3 cm) piece of muslin for the head and sewing thread to match
* face stamp and any dye ink pad or supplies to transfer the face template for placement on the muslin for the face

Bead Supplies

* size 6 or 8 seed beads: two black for eye pupils and various colors for stitching the face to the head (Note: Colors should complement the fabrics you are using for the body and costume.)
* size 11 seed beads in a medium color such as gold, tan, or peach for the face, eyebrows, and nose; in a medium or dark color for the first row of the eyelids; eight in pure white for the eye highlights; and any desired color for the iris. (Note: Unless otherwise noted, all references to seed beads in this chapter are to size 11.)
* size 14 seed beads, bugle beads, or pips (tiny bugle beads) for the lips and creative beading areas
* size 1 (3 mm) bugle beads in two or three colors for fill (optional)
* 3 or 4 mm sequins in colors that coordinate with the fabrics and beads used for the edge of the circle face
* 2 focal beads, no larger than 6 mm for the cheeks (optional)
* size D white or light tan Nymo beading thread or FireLine #6

Tools

* basic clothing, sewing, and beading kits (pages 12 and 13)

HEAD OUTLINE

Close-up of beaded head

1 Place your square of Pellon Stitch-n-Tear under your square of muslin, lining them up. Draw a 3" (7.6 cm) circle in the center of the square. Satin stitch with a width of at least ¼" (6 mm) around that outline so you have a solid border at the circle's edge. The stitching needs to be a firm border, as it gets turned under in the finishing steps. Satin stitch around a second time, on top of the previous stitching.

2 For the face, you can use any one of a variety of rubber stamps that are widely available and any dye ink pad (see tip box, this page). You can also draw a face on the fabric, use the template on page 118, or transfer a photo onto the muslin circle. If using a rubber stamp, press it onto the stamp pad and then onto the square of muslin. Even though you will be following the lines from the template or stamp, the face will look nothing like the stamp; they are merely guides for the placement of features. Be careful with the face placement so you do not lose the chin or forehead area. You will only be using this as a guide for the features.

3 Cut 1 yard (0.91 m) of Nymo or FireLine and run it through your beeswax several times. Run the FireLine through a tissue a couple of times to take off the oil. Thread your needle. Put a knot on one end of the single strand of thread. Starting behind the face (on the underside), insert your needle and come out on the front, at the four o'clock position, just inside the satin stitches. Pull your thread up through to the front, thus anchoring the knot in the back.

4 Slip on a sequin and then a seed bead. Slide them down the thread until the sequin is touching the muslin. At least half of your satin stitching should still be showing around the outermost edge. Push your needle back through the sequin, into, and then through, the muslin. Pull snugly. You have created a stopper bead with the seed bead, which holds the sequin in place. Now come up through the muslin again, fairly close to the first sequin unit (stack). Add a sequin and a bead. Turn around, skip the bead, and come back through the sequin again, to the back of the face. This sequin and bead unit should slightly overlap the first unit. Continue this rhythm all the way around the face, until the entire face circle has a sequin/beaded edge (figure a). Remember that you should be able to see half of the satin stitching all the way around.

(figure a)
Place a row of beads and sequins on the satin stitching.

5 If there is room between the facial features and the first sequined row, add another sequined row inside the first, so there are two rounds of sequin/bead units, as it makes the face fill in quicker. This time, you can try the size 6 or 8 seed beads with a stopper bead, a second row of sequins and beads, or a 3 or 4 mm cube bead or triangle bead with a stopper bead. The idea is that you are filling in as much as you can here. Remember, your working bead should just touch the previous bead, and the previous row, but not so tightly that it pushes the previous row out of line. Do not cut your thread.

Tip:

Anne Hesse uses a variety of rubber stamps for her faces that are widely available.

She used face stamp #2329F, from www.judikins.com, as the starting point for some work in this chapter. Two of her other favorites are #005032, Spirit of Soleil, from www.stampotique.com, and #4467-T, Facial Features, from www.100proofpress.com.

FEATURE OUTLINES

1 Select a seed bead color that is not too dark and not too pale. You would do well to use gold, tan, or peach for the eyebrow and nose outlines. As you look at your beaded face, beginning at the outermost edge of the eyebrow on the face's right side, bring your needle up from the back.

2 Thread on seven beads, slide them down the thread and lay them over the eyebrow line. Snug them up and, at the end of the seventh bead, push your needle into the fabric and pull through to the back side. Snug it up. If you look at your beads now, you will notice they form a straight line instead of the curve of the eyebrow. You will adjust this with couching.

3 Ensure your beads are firm against the fabric. With your finger, push them to make the curved shape. Still keeping the beads taut and holding them in position, bring your needle up through the fabric, between the two middle beads in the row. Draw the thread through so the thread can go over the top of the row and then be inserted back into the face (right side) of the fabric on

the opposite side of where it came up. Push the needle into and through the fabric to the back (figure b). Pull the thread firmly. The beads will curve, following the brow line. If you need to repeat this couching at another bead, it is perfectly fine to do so. Couch as many times as you need to get the curve you want.

(figure b)
Couch beads on the eyebrows.

4 Insert your needle from underneath, through the muslin, and into bead #4 of the original seven. Pull your thread through this bead and the remaining beads (5, 6, and 7). This process is called backstitching, which locks the beads in place. You should do this each time you sew a row of beads on, whether you have sewn three beads or seven. It reinforces the beading, holds your beads firmly, and gives you a starting point to begin your next stitch.

5 Slip on another seven beads. Your needle is already on the front side of your fabric. At this point, you will probably be rounding the curve where the brow begins the nose line. Do not forget to couch as you need to, if you want to keep the line in position. After you add the seven new beads, again lay them over the stamped line and insert your needle toward the underneath of the face. Pull the needle and thread through. Backstitch at the fourth bead and add more beads. Repeat, adding beads and backstitching, until you finish the nose line.

Tip:

- - - - - - - - - - - - - -

It is fine if your thread has to travel across the back of the muslin at this point. In fact, it is desirable, as criss-crossed threads build stability in to the piece and give it a bit more reinforcement.

Tip:

- - - - - - - - - - - - - -

You will not always begin with seven beads. Consider the length of the line you want to follow: it may allow only three or four beads, sometimes five beads.

6 Bead a short curvy line at the bottom edge of the nose, perpendicular to the existing beaded line of the nose and extending beyond both sides of the nose line (figure c).

(figure c)
Suggest the bottom of the nose with a short beaded line.

7 Looking at the front of the face, bring your threaded needle back up to the inside edge of the left eyebrow and bead this line. Remember to backstitch and couch as necessary. If you begin to run out of beading thread, you will need to knot off and rethread your needle to continue. Be sure your needle is on the underside of the beaded face. Being careful that the needle does not penetrate to the front side, gently slide your needle through the stitch and tear a few times. Take a short stitch and, just before pulling tightly, put your needle through the loop twice before pulling firmly. Repeat this knot two more times and then cut off the excess thread. Cut a new length of thread, wax it, clean it if you are using FireLine, knot an end and begin again, entering from the underside of the beaded face.

8 You will bead the lips the same way you have been working. You can use seed beads or, for an interesting look, try tiny bugle beads, called pips. If you decide to use seed beads, try using size 14 to keep the mouth from becoming too large. You may also use half bugles to create the mouth. Insert your needle from back to front of the muslin and follow the outline of the mouth. Now fill in the interior space (figure d).

(figure d)
Outline the mouth and then fill it in.

9 The eyes are next. During each step of this process, whatever you do on one eye should immediately be done on the other eye. There is a very small area for an eye, so move everything up a bit above the actual lines. The first row will be considered eye shadow and will define the lid. Use a medium to dark color for this. If you use a color that is too light, your eye will look like it has no lid. On the left eye, beginning a little lower than the actual line (about two or three beads lower) at the inside corner of the eye, string a line of seed beads to follow an imaginary curved line around the top of the eye that ends a little lower than the real line (again by about two or three beads) at the outer corner. Couch and backstitch as needed. Now go to the other eye and repeat the same row.

10 Stay at this second eye and add a pure white size 11 seed bead, a black size 8 bead, and another white size 11 seed bead in the middle of the curve of the lid, at the highest point. You want these beads to fit snugly together and to touch the line of the lid. Repeat this step on the opposite eye. You have just beaded the pupil and the highlights.

11 Stay at this eye (the first one you beaded) and decide what color you want the iris to be. Bead a semi-circle of the iris color around the highlights and pupil, beginning at the left edge of the white bead and just below the lid. This first bead should touch the white bead and one of the lid beads. Work your way around the white, black, and last white bead, ending at the lid. Anchor your work by couching and backstitching. Repeat for the other eye

(figure e)
Couch beads for the iris after applying the pupil and highlights.

12 Using a light peach or pale pink seed bead, bead from just inside one lid end to the other lid end of the same eye. This will mark the lower eyelid. If you have any remaining space in the interior of the eye, fill it in with white beads. Repeat this process for the other eye. This line should be straight across and touch the bottom of the iris.

(figure f)
Wendy Ness used bold colors to create this
beaded head.

COMPLETING THE FACE

It is now time for creative play. The most important ways to make each face individual and unique is to pay attention to—and change—three things: the direction of your beads, the color of your beads, and the size and type of your beads. If you keep this in mind as you work the rest of your face, you will truly have one that is one-of-a-kind. Here are several suggestions for filling in a face.

Wedges

Imagine the doll's face is a wheel. Visually divide this wheel by imagining the spokes. Each pie-shaped wedge can be treated differently by changing the type or size of beads, colors, and direction of placement (figure f). For example, in one wedge, try using bugle beads. In the area next to the bugle beads, create an area of short stacks (sequin and stop bead). Try using rows of seed beads (or any type of bead) for another wedge: create a pattern by repeating the same colors on each row within the wedge. Next to this wedge, use bugles again, in a different direction than the one previously done. There is no end to the ways you can fill these voids.

Cheek Blush

Another way to begin to creatively complete the rest of the face is to add rows of blush or light rose seed or bugle beads to make the cheeks stand out (figure g). Beginning under the eye, string on beads that follow the curve of the bottom lid. On each subsequent row, decrease the amount of beads by one. For example, the first row may have eight beads in it. The next row, which will be beaded below this first row, will have seven beads in it. Continue down until you have a row with only three beads in it. As you bead each row, center it under the row above it. You will form a sort of triangle of blush. If you are trying to design a beaded face for a clown, this is wonderful if you use bright red beads!

two on the left side of the doll's face. Play for a while by laying the beads onto the doll's face to see what they will look like before actually stitching them on.

(figure h)
Anne Hesse used fish-shaped beads on the cheeks of her doll.

(figure g)
Patti Medaris Culea made a realistic head by using flesh-colored beads.

Focal Beads

Yet another way to fill in the face is to use an interesting focal bead in the cheek area. Anne Hesse applies fill asymmetrically. She only uses one focal bead on one side of the face. You may, of course, choose to do the same to the other side of the face as well. Select a flower bead or some bead that may work with your theme; for example, fish beads are used for Anne's beaded mermaid (figure h). In this instance, the treatment is asymmetrical by using one fish on the right and

Fill Patterns

Still another way to fill in the space is to create a design with your beads. You can make spirals on one side of the face and stripes on the other side. To make a spiral, simply string on one color of beads. Begin at the outside of the spiral and curve around and to the inside as you add more beads. You will need to couch and backstitch quite a lot to maintain the shape. As you are curving the beads around, be sure to leave enough space between each row to add another row of beads of another color. That way, the spiral is clearly evident. This will become a major focal area. Use your imagination to create unusual and prominent designs.

FINISHING THE FACE

1 When you have completely finished beading your face, bring your needle through to the back side and knot it off several times. Trim that last thread. Place the beaded face flat on a table and smooth it out. Leaving ½" (1.3 cm) of the muslin and Stitch Tear surrounding the face, cut off the excess. You will have the beaded face with ½" (1.3 cm) of fabric around it. Gently tear the Stitch Tear off the back of this ½" (1.3 cm) area. It should pull off easily. If not, carefully trim it off close to the satin stitches, being careful not to nip the stitching (figure i).

2 Finger-press the remaining muslin toward the back. Fold the satin-stitched edging toward the back as well, so that the sequins on the outermost row form a scalloped edge.

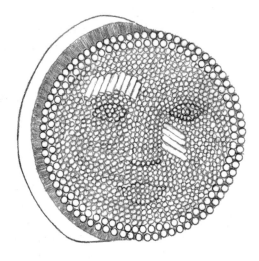

(figure i)
Trim off excess muslin outside the beaded outline.

3 You can sew this face directly on to your doll head or you can create a pancake head, as explained in the next section.

Tip:

As you are nearing the completion of the face, you will notice that the beads are beginning to pack more tightly together. Do not try to force in extra beads unless you have large gaps. If you try to force in extra beads, they will begin to overlap and your face will have ridges. In many cases, where it looks like you have a large opening, one bead will do the trick!

CREATING A PANCAKE HEAD

1 Take the rectangular piece of fabric and fold it lengthwise, with right sides together. Draw a circle that's 3" (7.6 cm) across and stitch through both layers, entirely around the circle (figure j, left). Trim off the excess, leaving a ¼" (6 mm) seam allowance.

2 Make a 1" (2.5 cm) slit in the middle of one side, being careful not to cut through the other side. Turn and stuff very lightly (figure j, right). Stitch the opening closed.

(figure j)
Stitch a 3" (7.6 cm) circle on the doubled fabric.

3 Take the beaded face and place it against this little pillow on the side with the opening. Wax, thread, and knot an end of your beading thread. Beginning at the pillow seam, sew through the seam and the edge of the beaded face, just behind a sequin in the outermost row. Remember to keep finger-pressing the extra fabric on the face to the underside of the beadwork. Choose one color of size 6 or 8 bead and one color of a seed bead. Bring your needle and thread completely through, add your larger bead and your stopper bead, go back through the larger bead, through the front of the beaded face at the folded edge behind the sequin, and through the pillow. Repeat this process of connecting the face to the head with beads until the entire face has been attached (figure k).

(figure k)
Side of beaded head made by Patti Medaris Culea

4 With a needle and sewing thread, hand stitch this entire head to the neck of the doll body. Leave some neck showing, but not enough to make the doll look goose-necked. Be careful not to pull your stitches too tight or the beaded face could be pulled into odd positions. Cover the back of the head entirely with doll hair, mohair, yarn, a turban, or beads.

BEADED HAIR

1 Collect a large variety of wonderful beads. If you have chosen a theme such as a mermaid, try to find some fish beads, or some beads that represent your particular theme. This is a great example of continuity of theme.

2 Wax and knot a length of beading thread. Thread your needle and then anchor your knot into the head, close to the bottom of the head and the top of the neck.

3 Stack as many delicious beads as desired for a lock of hair and then use a stopper bead. Turn around and sew back up through the beads.

4 Insert the needle into the head fabric, and come out at a new place. You are making beaded fringe, which allows the beads to be loose and create movement. Continue to make beaded fringes from the bottom to the top of the head, making the fringes shorter and shorter as you approach the very top.

Tip:

Repetition is one of Anne Hesse's favorite elements of art and she believes it's the most effective one. Other areas of her mermaid were also heavily embellished.

She used additional flukes for the shoulder caps. Anne always saves time by stitching parts together with beads in much the same way that the face was stitched to the pancake head (see Creating a Pancake Head, page 64). At the wrists, she layered rows of different beads. On the shoulders, she stitched with sequin and bead units to anchor the two flukes to the arm and then created a different pattern to anchor the two flukes together at the shoulder edges. The most important use of repetition was the flukes that were used as the hands.

Anne created a piece of fabric using snippets of material that she sewed together by free motion. These were used for the large fluke at the bottom of the tail and attached, again, by stitching with beads. She repeated the use of the free-motioned fabric just above the beaded wrists.

Continuity is another way to make your pieces cohesive. Two more large flukes were sewn on to the doll body as a jacket of sorts.

Anne used short stacks and a different set of beads, but the beads used throughout were already on the doll, in the hair. Again, repetition and continuity of materials and theme are essential for a refined piece of artwork.

Close-up of hands

Tip:

Anne says that often in her designs, she needs to be aware of "embellishing too much." Does the work become top heavy? Bottom heavy? Is there a flow in the design or is there too much for the eye to take in? Adding more can often be confusing and, ultimately, the undoing of a finely crafted doll. Take measure of the pieces you work on, leaving them for a day or so. "Go back and re-examine your work and the direction you are planning for the rest of the piece. Listen to your gut feeling and go with it," she says.

Anne considers beading to be one of the most meditative parts of her life. When she is beading and her focus is totally on what she is doing, her brain can rest. There is renewed energy and space then for new ideas to emerge. She wishes that each of you can find the peace and joy in bead embroidery that she has.

Simple bead embroidery on a doll by Jill Maas

GALLERY

Maddison

DI MCDONALD

The artist writes:

I chose the wonderful basic beginner's pattern from Patti's first book (*Creative Cloth Doll Making*; see Resources, page 121), changed the joints in the arms, and made separate hands. As time goes by, my taste in color seems to be changing, and right now I enjoy using more muted colors. Maddison is dressed in purples, muted pinks, and chartreuse.

Tyvek roses were placed on the Tyvek headdress and shoes, and Tyvek beads adorn the edges of her pantaloons. Maddison's shoes are beaded one by one. Her headdress and clothing are randomly beaded. Her torso was embellished with bead embroidery techniques using strings of beads on the back and front.

I enjoyed making this doll. She came together very easily and quickly until I got to the face. For some reason I thought I needed to make her face really funky and just couldn't get it right. I ended up putting Maddison on a shelf for a week until I came to the realization that it was okay for me to "just be me" and give her a "Di McDonald" face. There are always lessons for me to learn with the creation of every doll. What a wonderful journey I am on.

Olivine, the Forest Princess

KANDRA NORSIGIAN

The artist writes:

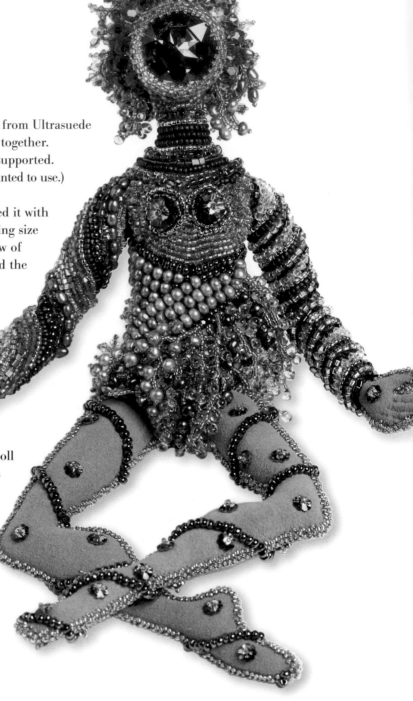

After shrinking the pattern by half, I cut the pieces from Ultrasuede and filled them with stuffing as I hand sewed them together. A dowel was inserted in the body to keep the head supported. (I knew her head would be heavy due to the beads I wanted to use.)

A large crystal rivoli was used for her face. I attached it with tacky tape then did one row of bead embroidery using size 11 seed beads. Peyote stitch was used on the one row of bead embroidery and was decreased so it would hold the crystal in place.

After drawing a design on the body, I started bead embroidering using size 8 triangle beads, 11s, 15s, and several other sizes and shapes. Beaded fringe became hair and was added to her waist.

When I teach beaded doll classes I have everyone start with the face. I believe this lets the doll dictate where to go next. Each segment of the doll's embellishment rises from what has gone before.

Fleur de Lace

WENDY NESS

The artist writes:

Maybe it's the painter in me, but I have a thing for the human figure, and I particularly love hands and feet. To create a more graceful foot, I increased the arch in the bottom of the foot pattern and wired the toes so that I could shape the feet. Her ankles and the palms of her hands have also been needle sculpted to give a more lifelike impression.

The body was made from white cotton Pimatex and the face was done as an applied cotton/Lycra skin, which was stuffed and then needle sculpted. I used my Jo Sonja's acrylics to mix a skin color into which I added Pale Gold, which gives her skin a slight shimmer. After I painted all her body parts, I strung her arms and legs together at the joints with wooden beads over which I wrapped and glued a range of flesh-colored seed beads. I glued a plastic straw inside each of the wooden beads so that the wrapped threads would not get worn away with the movement of her joints.

Once she was strung together, I pinned drifts of white floral lace over her body until I was happy with their position. I used my Jo Sonja's acrylics to paint the flower motifs, over which I dry-brushed Pale Gold. Various flowers, scrolls, and leaves were embroidered with seed beads before gluing each motif to her body. For a special touch, I had some beautiful Czech crystals that I glued randomly over her lace-encrusted body. Finally, I added some more paint to her bare skin with swirls and comma-strokes of Gold. The final effect is quite rich yet rather subtle as the beading is not excessive.

Lagoon Girl

SHARON MANN

The artist writes:

Lagoon Girl incorporates beading, crochet, embroidery stitches, and machine and hand sewing. Her color scheme of blues and greens suits her personality because she lives near the water. The face is made with a black felt oval, simply embroidered with the buttonhole stitch and straight stitch for the nose and eyes. A green-fringed novelty yarn is used for her arms and bodice to give the look of seaweed or lagoon grass. To complete the bodice, beads are strung between the neck and waist. Her head design is only beads and a crocheted cap (because hair would tangle in the water). The hands are machine sewn right-side out, the fabric trimmed very close to the seam, and then embroidered with the button-hole stitch to give more of a webbed look. Lagoon Girl's boots are for after her swim. They are made of felt and embellished bead techniques; a variety of bead sizes is used for decoration. The buttonhole stitch finishes off the top of the boots.

Haute Couture

VALÉRIE LEGRAND-PRENEY

The artist writes:

Making a doll is always a challenge—which grows even more so when Patti proposes a creation! When I have an inspiration, it is enough for me to write down some ideas and draw a few sketches. Then it is a true adventure to choose the materials. Sometimes it is the material that brings an idea to me. For this doll, I wanted to simplify the bottom of the body to give her a silhouette of sheath dress in order to focus on the costume. I was inspired by the paintings of Gustav Klimt when creating a gilded dress. I applied woven wire tubing (like skeleton's leaves), silk circles, and triangles covered with beads and sequins. The silk ballerina slippers are bordered with organza ribbons and beads. The tulle hairstyle is attached with organza beaded flowers.

Chapter 4

Enhancing the Figure

Wood Elf

BY LAURA MCCABE

Laura McCabe comes from a background in historical costume, anthropology, and bead weaving, but this book marks her first attempt at doll making. It was an interesting and eye-opening journey for her to apply her skills to the art of dolls.

She discovered, to her surprise, that the embellishment of a doll is its own journey. As the doll takes on its own personality, it dictates the manner in which it should be embellished. She was amazed to realize by the end that her doll had turned in to something she had never expected. The doll did, in a subtle way, determine her own creation.

In this chapter, Laura provides specific step-by-step instructions on how to create a variety of embellishments for flora forms that incorporate both seed beads and crystals, as well as Czech and German pressed glass, and freshwater pearls. These forms can then be used as you wish to embellish simple doll clothing that is made by cutting and draping. It is her hope that by offering you a slightly alternative perspective on beading and embellishing cloth dolls, that she provides you with the knowledge and information that will allow you to continue on your own journey in to the fascinating world of doll making.

Materials

✳ Basic Doll Body (page 14)

✳ scraps of soft leather in two colors: 6" (15.2 cm) square for the bodice, 6" (15.2 cm) square for the hat, 3" x 6" (7.6 x 15.2 cm) for a pair of shoes, and 12" x 18" (30.5 x 45.7 cm) for the skirt

Tools

✳ basic clothing, sewing and beading kits (pages 12 and 13)

✳ size 12 glover's needle

Bead Supplies

✳ one gross each of bicone crystals in 3 mm or 4 mm for buds, 3 mm for the berries, and 4 mm for Basic Flower #1, Basic Flower #2, and Bud bezel embellishment

✳ five 6 mm crystal lentil beads for the Embroidered Star Flower

✳ eleven 12 mm rivoli crystals for the linked cabochon belt

✳ 18 mm rivoli crystals for each starburst (embellished bezeled rivoli crystal)

✳ fifteen 4 mm or 6 mm freshwater pearls in two colors for the berries

✳ 1 gram of size 15 Japanese seed beads for every color desired for each starburst (embellished bezeled rivoli crystal)

✳ 5 grams each of size 11 Miyuki Delica seed beads in two colors for a bezeled rivoli crystal and linking cabochons to create chains

✳ 5 grams of size 11 seed beads for the Basic Bud, Basic Flower #1, Basic Flower #2, Beaded Flower, Embroidered Star Flower, Berries on a Stalk, and Bud bezel embellishment

✳ 4 mm or 6 mm flat bead for each Embroidered Star Flower

✳ 5 grams of size 15 silver or gold Czech charlottes for a bezeled rivoli crystal and picot embellishment for a bezel

✳ 10 grams of size 15 seed beads in five colors for the Basic Bud, Basic Flower #1, Basic Flower #2, Beaded Flower, Embroidered Star Flower, Berries on a Stalk, bezeled rivoli crystal, picot and Bud bezel embellishments, and linking cabochons

✳ 4 mm rondelle for each Basic Flower #1 and Basic Flower #2

✳ 6 mm or 8 mm center-drilled pressed glass flower for each Basic Flower #1 and Basic Flower #2

✳ size D Nymo thread in color to match leather

✳ size 12 English beading needle for the bezeling

Close-up of head with hat

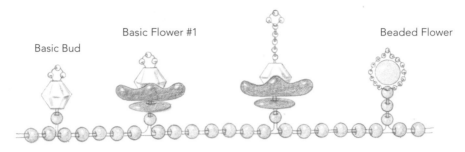

Basic Bud

Basic Flower #1

Basic Flower #2

Beaded Flower

(figure a)
Stack beads to make basic shapes. The basic bud is the simplest of flower forms.

MAKING THE CLOTHING

To make the clothing for the doll, drape the leather on the doll and decide on the length you want for the skirt. Cut this in an A-line skirt shape. Cut two of these. Sew the two pieces together, wrong sides together. Use a whip stitch, Nymo thread, and a leather needle. Leave a seam open at the top to make it easier to slip the skirt on to the doll after the beading is completed.

The bodice is made from a large triangle of leather. By draping the points of the upside-down triangle over the shoulders, the wide, straight edge at the top of the triangle goes across the front of the neck, over the shoulders, and down the back. There is a seam where the opposite ends of the edge meet along the center back to create a poncho of sorts. Then the remaining sides of the triangle are seamed underneath the arms, to leave armholes and create a fitted, bodice-style garment. The hat and shoes were cut to the shape and then stitched by hand. Beadwork was added using the techniques in this chapter.

When it comes to beaded flower forms, there are almost infinite possibilities in the realm of beadwork. This chapter will provide you with four basic forms, intended as starting points from which your imagination is the limit.

BASIC BUD

1 Coming out of the beadwork or off the fabric surface with a doubled strand of FireLine, pick up a size 11 seed bead, a 4 mm bicone crystal, and three size 15 seed beads (figure a).

2 Go back through the bicone crystal and the size 11 bead and back into the beadwork or fabric surface to create a picot (triangle of three beads with the size 15 beads).

BASIC FLOWER #1

Both of the basic flower forms (#1 and #2) are simply more advanced versions of the basic bud. They are created by stacking beads upon each other, resulting in beaded forms that look like small flowers.

1 Coming out of the beadwork or off the fabric surface with a doubled strand of FireLine, pick up a size 11 seed bead, a 4 mm rondelle, a 6 mm or 8 mm center-drilled pressed glass flower, a 4 mm bicone crystal, and three size 15 seed beads (figure a).

2 Go back through the 4 mm crystal, the pressed glass flower, the rondelle, and the size 11 bead, and back into the beadwork or fabric surface to create a picot.

BASIC FLOWER #2

The second basic flower form is merely a variation on the first, Basic Flower #1. This time, you use seed beads to create a pistil-like center extending out from the flower.

1 Coming out of the beadwork or off the fabric surface with a doubled strand of FireLine, pick up a size 11 seed bead, a 4 mm rondelle, a 6 mm or 8 mm center-drilled pressed-glass flower, a 4 mm bicone crystal, five size 15 seed beads of color A, and three more size 15 beads of a second color (color B) (figure a).

2 Go back through the five color A size 15 beads, the 4 mm crystal, the pressed-glass flower, the rondelle, the size 11 bead, and back in to the beadwork or fabric surface to create a picot (triangle of three beads with the color B size 15 beads).

BEADED FLOWER

The beaded flower is a simpler version of the Embroidered Star Flower. It is shown on page 80 with a 6 mm crystal lentil bead center, but can be made with a pearl or pressed-glass bead center.

1 Coming out of the beadwork or off the fabric surface with a doubled strand of FireLine, pick up three size 11 seed beads, a 6 mm crystal lentil bead, and three size 15 seed beads (figure a).

2 Go back through the crystal to create a picot (triangle of three beads with the size 15 beads).

3 Pick up seven size 15 beads and, circling around the crystal, go back through all three beads in the picot, one bead at a time. This finishes one side of the flower.

4 To finish the second side of the flower, pick up seven more size 15 beads, go back down through the flower stem (three size 11 beads below the crystal), and back into the beadwork or fabric surface.

Tip:

English beading needles are better quality and slightly smaller than the Indian pony needles.

Close-up of embroidered star flower

EMBROIDERED STAR FLOWER

1 Collect a 4 mm or 6 mm flat bead, size 15 seed beads in five colors (A, B, C, D, and F), and size 11 seed beads in another color (color E).

2 Coming off the fabric surface with a single strand of FireLine, pick up the flat bead (for the flower center). Stitch back down into the fabric surface, on the opposite side of the bead, to hold it flat against the surface. This is the first pass.

3 Come back up through the textile at the same place that you started. Go back through the bead again for the second pass, but do not go back down into the textile a second time. Instead, pick up three size 15 beads, in an A-B-A color sequence (figure b).

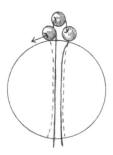

(figure b)
Anchor accent bead to fabric.

4 Go back through the flat, center bead to create a picot (triangle of three beads with the size 15 beads). Do not go into the fabric. This is the third pass. Pick up three more size 15 beads (also in an A-B-A color sequence), and go back through the flat bead toward the first picot. This is the fourth pass (figure c).

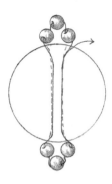

(figure c)
Create a picot with size 15 seed beads.

5 Go through all three beads in the first picot and pick up seven or nine size 15 beads in a B-A-B-A-B-A-B color sequence. The number of beads you pick up depends on the size of the center bead you used and the number of size 15 beads it will take to fill in the space around the bead between the picots). Circling around the center bead, go back through all three beads in the second picot, one bead at a time (figure d).

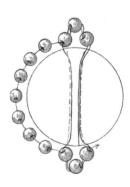

(figure d)
Circle half the center bead with seed beads.

6 Pick up seven more size 15 beads, in a B-A-B-A B A-B color sequence, and go back up through the first two size 15 beads in the first picot (figure e).

(figure e)
Circle remaining side of center bead with seed beads.

7 Pick up a color C size 15 bead, and go through the next color B bead. Continue in this manner all the way around the center bead to the second picot. Go through the middle bead of the picot and then continue adding color C beads around to the first picot. You are doing peyote stitch but, by utilizing the color A and B beads, it is very easy to see where the needle should go.

8 Once you have completed one round of peyote stitch with the color C beads and have gone back through the top color B bead in the first picot, step up through the first color C bead (figure f).

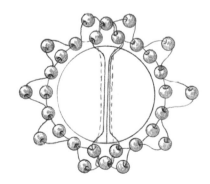

(figure f)
Step up through the first color C bead.

9 You are now ready to create the petals. To form a petal, pick up a size 15 color D bead, a size 11 color E bead, and three size 15 color F beads.

10 Go back through the color E bead (to form a picot with the color F beads). Pick up one more color D bead and go through the next color C bead. This forms one petal. Continue in this manner, creating one petal between every color C bead. Once you have completed the round, go up through the size 15 color D bead, the size 11 color E bead and the first two size 15 color F beads in the first petal of the flower (figure g).

11 Stitch into the fabric surface, come back up again and go through the same bead a second time and back into the fabric surface.

12 On the underside of the fabric surface, skip over to the next petal picot, come up through the fabric surface (to the right side) and go through the middle bead in the picot (figure h). Continue in this manner until all petal picots have been stitched down. Knot off the thread with a double half hitch (page 26) on the back side of the fabric before cutting the thread. (Note: Each round of the illustration is shown in a different color. Round colors do not represent a change in actual bead color.)

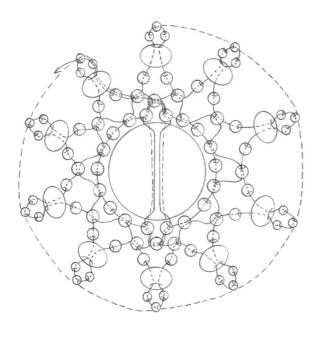

(figure g)
Create beaded petals.

(figure h)
Stitch down the petal picots.

Rounds colored for identification only

BERRIES ON A STALK

1 Collect size 11 seed beads, 4 mm or 6 mm pearls, 3 mm bicone crystals, and size 15 seed beads. Coming out of the beadwork or fabric surface with a doubled strand of FireLine, string up thirteen size 11 beads. Pick up a pearl, a bicone crystal, and three size 15 beads. Go back through the crystal and pearl to create a picot (triangle of the size 15 beads), and then into the last size 11 bead (figure i). Be sure to pull tight on your working thread. This is the stalk and berry at the end of the stalk.

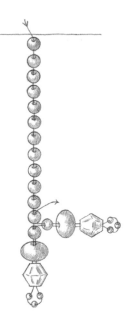

(figure j)
Add beads on the stalk for a berry.

(figure i)
Create a picot and return through top beads.

2 Pick up a size 11 bead, a pearl, a bicone crystal, and three size 15 beads. Go back through the crystal and pearl, and the size 11 bead, and then into the next size 11 bead on the berry stalk to start the third berry (figure j). The intent is to crowd the berries on the stalk, like a cluster of grapes.

Close-up of a berry cluster

3 Continue adding berries until you have reached the top of the size 11 beads, then weave the thread back into the fabric surface.

Close-up of bezeled rivoli starburst on the doll's chest

OPEN-BACK BEZELING FOR POINT-BACK AND IRREGULAR-BACK RIVOLI CRYSTALS OR STONES

Bezeling is the process of encasing a rivoli crystal or stone in a setting. This can be done with metal or a variety of other materials. In this case, you will be weaving the bezel from seed beads with tubular peyote stitch. Being able to create open-back bezels is highly advantageous as it allows you to work with point-backs or irregular, nonflat back rivolis.

1 Collect Miyuki Delica size 11 seed beads, a rivoli (any size), size 15 Japanese seed beads, and size 15 charlottes. String up a wingspan (about 5' [1.5 m]) of single threaded FireLine on a size 12 English beading needle. Wax the thread well, if desired. Pick up enough Delicas to encircle the widest point of your rivoli. The circle of Delicas should be a perfect fit: not too loose, not too tight. You also want an even number of beads. If it works out that a perfect fit is an odd number, then always add an additional bead, rather than take one bead off the thread. The chart on the following page 29 provides the counts for some basic rivolis. Tie the thread ends together with a square knot (page 29) to form a circle of beads. Leave about 15" (38.1 cm) of thread as a tail.

Tip:

Beading experts all agree that waxing thread helps prevent knots and kinks. The only difference of opinion comes when working on fabric. Some still use beeswax, others feel it will leave a mess on the fabric. Others prefer a micro-crystalline thread conditioner or Thread Heaven. Beeswax proponents say that the other conditioners can leave a fine oil on fabric. Experiment, and then make your own decision.

2 Tie the thread ends together with a square knot to form a circle of beads. Leave about 15" (38.1 cm) of thread as a tail. You can use this long tail to join the piece to fabric or other beads.

3 Now you will make a base (underside) for the rivoli. Using your working thread, go through two or three Delicas to hide the knot inside a bead, then begin

Guidelines for Bezeling Rivoli Crystals

RIVOLI SIZE	DELICAS in Initial Circle (*step 1*)	ROWS Peyote Stitching with Delicas	Beads on BACK (underside) of Rivoli (*steps 3–5*)	Beads on FRONT of Rivoli (*steps 6–7*)
12 mm	30	1 row	1 row of size 15 seed beads / 1 row of charlottes	1 row of size 15 seed beads / 1 row of charlottes
14 mm	36	1 row	2 rows of size 15 seed beads / 1 row of charlottes	2 rows of size 15 seed beads / 1 row of charlottes
16 mm	40	1 row	2 rows of size 15 seed beads / 1 row of charlottes	3 rows of size 15 seed beads / 1 row of charlottes
18 mm	46	1 row	2 rows of size 15 seed beads / 1 row of charlottes	3 rows of size 15 seed beads / 1 row of charlottes

NOTE: *The number of seed beads and rows may vary, depending on your tension when working with the beads. Vary the number of Delicas and the number of rows as necessary to create a nice, tight fit to the rivoli.*

peyote stitching (page 27) with Delicas, working one row off of the original circle. Once you begin stitching into the initial circle the beads will shift around, so actually there are three rows of peyote. Peyote is counted on the diagonal, so if you run a needle through the ring on the diagonal, you will count three rows. At the end of the row, you will need to step up (page 26) to begin your next row.

4 Switch to size 15 Japanese seed beads. Peyote stitch one to three more rows using these beads. You may stay with the same color throughout or switch to a new color for each new row. Whether you do one, two, or three rows depends on your tension and the size of the rivoli. You will need more rows if your tension is tight or the rivoli is large. To check the fit, pop the rivoli in place and you will be able to get an idea as to whether or not the additional rows are necessary. The rows need to trap the edges of the rivoli, and create a "frame" without visually overpowering the rivoli.

5 Do the final row with size 15 charlottes. The back (underside) is now complete.

6 Needle up to the top, first (outermost) row of Delicas. Pop the rivoli in to the bezel you have created. Hold it in place as you work on top of the rivoli to securely capture it in the following manner: Work one to three rows of size 15 Japanese seed beads, depending on rivoli size and thread tension.

7 Finish off with size 15 charlottes, in peyote stitch, for the last row.

8 Once you have finished the last row of charlottes, half hitch a couple times to knot off before cutting your thread. At this point you have successfully bezeled the rivoli. This bezeled piece can be stitched directly to your doll or fabric surface or further embellished. You can also create a number of these bezeled rivolis or stones and then link them together to create a belt (see Linking Cabochons to Create Chains, page 87).

BEZEL EMBELLISHMENT

Picots

The most basic embellishment off a bezel is simple bead picots. Usually it is best to do these picots with size 15 seed beads or size 15 charlottes. This technique will provide a simple, but lovely, picot edge to your bezel. This picot stitch can be done in one row or multiple rows on the bezel, depending on the look you desire.

1 Use FireLine thread, doubled or single, as desired. Coming out of a bead in any row of the peyote stitching in the bezel, pick up three size 15 seed beads.

2 Go into the next bead in the same row of the bezel (figure k).

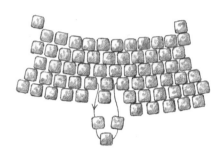

(figure k)
Anchor picots in any row of the bezel.

Bud

This bezel embellishment is very much like the Basic Bud on page 78.

1 With a strand of FireLine, come out of a bead in any row of the peyote stitching in the bezel. Pick up a size 11 seed bead, a 3 mm or 4 mm bicone crystal, and three size 15 Japanese seed beads.

2 Go back through the bicone crystal and the size 11 seed bead, toward the bezel base (figure l).

3 Go into the next bead in the same row of the bezel. Pull tight on the thread to create a stiff embellishment.

(figure l)
Add basic buds rather than picots.

Tip:

All of the dimensional embellishment described in this chapter can be worked off of a peyote-stitch bezel. By coming out of a bead in a bezel row, creating an embellishment, and going back into the next bead in the same bezel row, the embellishment will sit over the ditch (the space between adjacent beads in a row).

LINKING CABOCHONS TO CREATE CHAINS

Close-up of a cabochon belt with picot-embellished bezels

You can link open-back bezeled stones beautifully to create a chain of rivoli crystals that work well as a bracelet, necklace, or belt. The first step in this process is to create a number of open-back bezeled rivolis (page 84). Once these are complete, you are ready to connect them.

If you desire embellishment on the rivolis, this should be done after all the rivolis have been linked.

1 Collect size 11 Miyuki Delica seed beads and bezeled and embellished rivoli or stones. Using a single strand of thread (the long thread tail left at the beginning of the bezeling), weave down to the center row of Delicas on the bezel. The center row is the row around with only one bead. If you look at the bezel, you will see there are two beads stacked on each other, then one bead, then two, then one. The single, unstacked, beads make up the center row. Coming out of a bead in this center row, pick up a size 11 Delica and go through the next Delica in the same bezel row (figure m).

(figure m)
Add a Delica to a bead in the center row.

2 Pick up another Delica, turn around and go back through the bead you just added (figure n). Weave back and forth in this manner until you have created a tab of the desired length.

(figure n)
Add another Delica for first row of tab.

3 Once your tab is the proper length, it will be zipped into the center row of the next bezeled rivoli. Zipping is accomplished by going back and forth from a bead in the tab to a bead in the center row of the next rivoli and back again (figure o). This creates an interlacing between the two rivolis, which, when pulled tight, zips the two pieces together seamlessly.

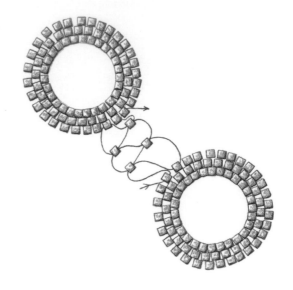

(figure o)
Zip the bezeled rivolis together.

4 Once you have connected the first two rivolis you are ready to weave through the Delicas on the second bezel, around the other far side of the second rivoli and create another tab to connect the next bezel. Continue on in this manner until all the rivolis have been linked.

GALLERY

Ysanne

VERA EVANS

The artist writes:

My inspiration for Ysanne came from the intense jewel-tone colors of summer flowers in the gardens my mother and mother-in-law tended to with great care every year. The beading of the doll was my favorite part. I started by making the thistle that Ysanne holds in her hand. It is a combination of peyote and fringe that is made into a strip then rolled to form the top of the thistle. A netting stitch covers a painted wooden bead for the base. The tulip-shaped flowers were made using Delicas and size 15s. A vine was created using peyote stitch, and the leaves and flowers were attached. The little berries are 4 mm miracle beads covered in size 15s. The final detail is her dragonfly. This is a pin I made several years ago. The dragonfly went perfectly with the color scheme and is pinned to her hand so I can remove it and still wear it myself.

Moresca

MICHELLE MEINHOLD

The artist writes:

I gained inspiration for Moresca from a book I received for my birthday. It had the most amazing artwork of fairies I had ever seen. There was a picture of a mermaid that I just fell in love with. Her hair was encrusted with pearls and jewels. That sparked my design. I think I was a magpie in a previous life because I find the sparkle of Swarovski crystals completely enchanting. Most of my beadwork is made with Austrian crystals. I used 3 mm and 4 mm bicones, cubes, rounds, vintage rivolis, and faceted lentils to bead the bodice and grapes. Using right-angle weave and the 3 mm bicones, I made individual grapes that I then wove into bunches that are attached to her shoulders. Her bodice was created by attaching the captured rivolis directly to her body and then embroidering the pearls and crystals in the empty spaces.

Size 15 seed beads and flat peyote stitch make up her wings and the grape leaves that are attached to her shoulders. To make her wings stiffer, I dipped them in Future floor acrylic and then dried them flat. The Future both stiffens them and also protects the dyed beads from fading.

Finally, my favorite part of Moresca was her hair. I used some of the leftover crystals, crystal grapes, a crystal grape leaf, a strand of pearls, and crystal head pins to embellish her hair. Moresca is ready for her debut on the stage at the festival for Dionysus, held each spring when the leaves begin to reappear on the vine.

Merlina, Water Queen

TERESA MALYON

The artist writes:

It took a while for me to decide if Merlina would be a mermaid or a fairy. Since my doll world is heavily populated with fairies, I took the plunge with her and had a swimmingly good time.

I used the wing pattern as her flukes and added the smaller flukes on top. I cut down another wing pattern to make a dorsal fin down her back. I cross-hatched the organza using two colors. I used aurora embroidery thread for sewing a basic pattern on each of the flukes, including her scaly layers, and beaded on top using a variety of different shaped aurora clear beads and crystals.

As we all know, during their creation, dolls take on their own personality and in Merlina's case, she evolved in to something quite regal. That's why I felt she needed a tiara and a staff to hold.

Titania, Queen of the Fairies

MARY CONNOLLY

The artist writes:

My inspiration for Titania was a pair of shoes in a magazine advertisement for stockings. I tore out the page and put it away thinking that one day I would make a pair of shoes like that for a fairy doll. So when I received an email from Patti asking me to participate in this book and I read the requirements, my first thought was of those shoes and that fairy.

I made the shoes first from a pattern by Pearl Moon. The shoes are beaded and have flower beads on beading wire so that they look like flowers on a stem. I beaded her bodice and the lace collar with silver seed beads and Swarovski crystals. I beaded around the neckline, skirt bottoms, and sleeves with various colors of pinks, silver, and clear seed beads. Around the bottom of the lower skirt I ruched a wired ribbon and sewed it on, then beaded with various beads, flowers, and butterflies.

Her wings are crystal organza stiffened with Visofix and with wire shaped to fit the wings. They have a bit of the material from the dress and some Angelina fiber trapped inside. Her crown is peyote beaded and has Swarovski crystals on the top. A pear-shaped crystal hangs down from silver beads in her hair.

Titania's mace is a piece of aluminum rod with a large Swarovski crystal wired in to the rod. It also has a starburst flower at the top. A garland of beads and flowers winds its way around the rod making the mace fit for a fairy queen.

Chapter 5

Wings

and

Things

Franalizia of the North Sea

BY PATTI MEDARIS CULEA

In this chapter, in addition to traditional beads, you will learn to make and use many types of synthetic fabrics to create your own unique beads. Essentially, all you need to do is gather the material and apply heat to slightly melt it into a bead form.

The mermaid in this chapter is designed from a combination of shimmering and glimmering elements. Her tail is created using batik fabric and beads. Synthetic organza creates the very light and shimmery beads used along the top edge of her tail. Her flukes, wings (yes, she's a fairy mermaid), and scales use a combination of peyote beadwork and fabrics. None of the techniques used on the mermaid are difficult, but they allow for individual touches and are enjoyable to make, so jump in and have fun!

Materials

- ✳ Basic Doll Body (page 14), upper body only (no legs) Note: Do not attach arms.
- ✳ ⅓ yard (0.31 m) of batik cotton for the tail, flukes, and scales
- ✳ ⅓ yard (0.31 m) of batik cotton in a contrasting color for the flukes and scales
- ✳ ¼ yard (0.23 m) of synthetic organza in each of three colors and one in white for the shoulders, base of the tail, beads, and waist
- ✳ plastic pellets to fill the tail
- ✳ variegated rayon or polyester sewing thread to match your color theme
- ✳ metallic sewing thread to match the variegated thread
- ✳ strong thread to match the tail color
- ✳ acrylic paint in a variety of colors for the organza beads
- ✳ embossing powders to match the organza beads
- ✳ tacky craft glue such as Crafter's Pick The Ultimate or Jones Tones Plexi Glue

Tools

- ✳ basic clothing, sewing, and beading kits (pages 12 and 13)
- ✳ wooden skewer (satay stick) for the organza beads
- ✳ size 12/80 metallic or top-stitch sewing machine needle
- ✳ hand-sewing needle: sharp or milliners
- ✳ dust mask for the organza beads
- ✳ heat or embossing gun for the organza beads
- ✳ candle and matches for the organza embellishments on tail and shoulders

Bead Supplies

- ✳ 10 grams each of size 11 Miyuki Delica seed beads in white and four more colors for the shells, bust, and crown
- ✳ 20 grams each of size 15 seed beads in three colors for the scales and flukes and one color for the bracelets
- ✳ 20 grams each of size 11 seed beads in the same three colors as the size 15 seed beads for the scales and flukes and one other color (to match the size 8 seed beads) for the bracelets
- ✳ 20 grams of size 8 seed beads for the bracelets
- ✳ 20 grams of size 11 pink seed beads for the coral
- ✳ size 11 x 5.5 mm crystal drops in four colors for the scales and flukes
- ✳ 3 mm bicone crystals: fifty in pink for the coral and two in pink for the pair of starfish
- ✳ 4 mm bicone crystals: twenty in each of four colors for the flukes and wings
- ✳ 10" (25.4 cm) strand of 4 mm freshwater pearls for the waist, coral on the bust, bracelets, and crown
- ✳ 1 gram of size 15 silver charlottes for the flukes and coral
- ✳ accent beads, such as small shells with holes in them, and other beads for the crown
- ✳ circular sequins in five to seven colors for the scales
- ✳ three colors of Micro Beads or no-sew beads
- ✳ 3 mm Hot-Fix (heat-set, iron-on) crystals in two or three colors for the flukes, belly button, and finishing the doll's body
- ✳ Nymo size B beading thread in color to match work
- ✳ one spool of 24-gauge beading wire

MERMAID TAIL

To get started on a mermaid, create an upper body, but do not attach the arms.

1 Trace one of each of the pattern pieces for the Mermaid Tail Front and Back (page 120) onto the wrong side of the batik cotton. Double the cotton, right sides together (figure a, left).

(figure a)
Trace, sew, and join the tail pieces.

2 Do not cut out the fabric shapes. Sew seam #1 on the Tail Back and seam #2 on the Tail Front. Cut out both tail pieces using pinking shears. The top edge of the tail should be cut with straight-edge scissors. Pin the front and back tail sections, right sides together. Sew along seam #3 from the top of the hip (widest part) down around the bottom of the tail (point) and back up to the top of the hip on the other side (figure a, right). Turn the piece right side out. (Note: All seam allowances for items in this chapter are ⅛" (3 mm) wide.)

3 Fill the tail to the dashed line found on the pattern pieces with fine plastic pellets. Place a small amount of stuffing on top of the pellets. Slip the tail onto the doll's upper body and pin it in place. Do not turn under the upper, raw edge of the tail. It will be covered later. With a small hand-sewing needle and strong thread, back-stitch the tail to the body. You don't need to be neat, as beads and scales will cover the stitches. Set the body aside for now.

Close-up of the tail

SCALES FOR THE TAIL

1 Trace the Scales pattern (page 118) onto the wrong side of two colors of batik fabric. You will need to trace a total of seven scale strips. Trace three on one batik fabric, and four on the contrasting batik fabric. Each finished strip will become a row on the mermaid's tail. Double the fabric, or place another color on the other side. Pin these right sides together. For each of the seven traced scales, sew along the scalloped edge (seam #4) and, at both ends, seams #5 and #6 (figure b). Cut out the shapes with pinking shears. Turn right side out and press the scales flat with an iron. Do not press open the seam allowances.

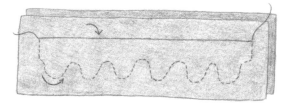

(figure b)
Sew together pairs of scales.

2 Now it is time to cross-stitch bead along the finished seam line of seam #4. Collect the size 15 and 11 seed beads, the crystal drops, sequins, FireLine thread, and a beading needle. Cut 1½ yards (1.37 m) of the FireLine and thread this in a size 10 or 12 beading needle. Place a knot in the single end.

3 Starting at the X marked on the pattern piece, push the needle from inside the scales to the outside where marked on the pattern to start the beading. Take a small stitch in the seam, and then come out close to the edge (figure c, left).

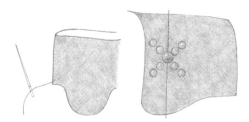

(figure c)
Straddle seam #4 with beaded cross-stitch edging.

4 Needle up two size 15 seed beads, one size 11 seed bead, and two size 15 seed beads (all of the beads are in one color). Diagonally cross the line of beads over finished seam #4, and push the needle through only the layer of fabric on the underside of the scale, close to the seam line. As you push the needle in, be careful to avoid catching the top fabric. Angle the needle up, on the underside of the scale and come out. You're making an X that straddles the seam line, so the needle must come out in a spot on the underside that's directly in line with the place you started the previous strand on the upper fabric layer. Needle up two size 15 seed beads and go in to the size 11 seed bead on the previous strand. Push the needle into the seam under the size 11 seed bead and come out the other side of the seam. Push the needle back into the size 11 seed bead and add two more size 15 seed beads. Angle down on the top side of the scale and push the needle into the fabric (figure c, right).

5 Continue creating the beaded cross-stitch until you come to the place marked at the bottom center of the scale on the pattern. Push the needle from the last bead added out of the fabric at this mark and add two size 15 seed beads, one size 11 seed bead, three size 15 seed beads, one crystal drop, and three size 15 seed beads. Skip the last three size 15 seed beads, the crystal drop, and the other three size 15 seed beads. Push the needle into the size 11 seed bead and the last two size 15 seed beads.

6 Anchor this cluster by pushing the needle into the seam, under the size 11 seed bead and coming out at the back (bottom fabric layer) of the scale. Needle up two size 15 seed beads and push the needle into the fabric then out about ¾" (1.9 cm) in from the fabric edge, directly in line with the drop cluster. Needle up a sequin and one size 11 seed bead. Skip the seed bead and push the needle into the sequin and into the fabric (figure d). Come out next to the size 15 seed bead above the crystal drop cluster.

(figure d)
Create a crystal drop cluster at the center of each scallop.

7 Continue steps 4, 5, and 6 until you come to the end of the strip (row). Anchor the thread in the seam line and cut the thread. Set the row of scales aside. With each set of scales, change the colors of the beads. The doll shown on page 96 starts with crystal at the bottom, then purple, blue, and pink. The other rows repeat in reverse: blue, purple, and then crystal. Set the scales aside for now.

WINGS, FLUKES, AND FINS

1 On the wrong side of a batik fabric trace two Wings, three Large Flukes, and four Small Fluke patterns (pages 118–119). Either double the fabric or pin a different batik fabric to the fabric with the tracings. Place the fabrics, right sides together.

2 With matching thread in your sewing machine, a lower stitch length (1.5 on a Bernina), and the fabric layers held together, sew from the opening at the top all the way around each fluke. On the wings, sew from the openings all the way around. Backstitch at the openings to keep the seams from splitting when turning each piece right side out. Cut out all pieces, clipping through the seam allowances at the curves. Turn right side out using a small pair of hemostats. Push out the curves of the wings and flukes by inserting the hemostats inside the turned fabric.

3 Place decorative machine threads in both the upper needle and bobbin of the sewing machine. Either free motion or topstitch along the inside of the flukes. Follow the guidelines on the wings. Be sure to leave small openings for the beading wire.

4 Without removing the wire from the spool, bend back the cut end and pinch it closed with either the needle-nose pliers or hemostats. Insert this end into a fluke where marked with a wire placement line. Measure the other end along the outside of the fluke, along the next closest wire placement line. Cut the wire to fit and bend back the cut end. Insert it into the fluke at the second line (figure e). Do this one more time, to wire the remaining lines on the fluke. Do the same with the wings and remaining flukes, following the markings on the pattern pieces.

(figure e)
Topstitch a decorative pattern on flukes and insert wire.

5 Collect the size 11 and 15 seed beads, crystal drops, 4 mm bicone crystals, charlottes (optional), FireLine thread, micro or no-sew beads, tacky craft glue, and size 12 beading needle. Cut the FireLine in 1½ yard (1.37 m) lengths. Thread the needle with the FireLine.

6 Place a knot in the single end of the FireLine. Insert the needle inside the top of a fluke and come out in a seam. Take a small stitch in the seam to anchor the thread.

7 Set the wings aside. Following the picot edging (page 28), edge the flukes until you get to a point. Work each point by following the instructions for the appropriate size of fluke.

Large Fluke: Coming from the back of the fabric or beadwork, push the needle through the second bead (the last bead added to the most recent picot), add a size 11 seed bead, a 4 mm bicone crystal, a size 11 seed bead, three size 15 seed beads, a crystal drop, and three size 15 seed beads. Skip the last three size 15 seed beads, the crystal drop, and the next three size 15 seed beads. Push the needle back through the size 11, 4 mm bicone crystal, two size 11 seed beads, and in to the fabric (figure f). Turn the needle around and go back

through the closest 11 seed bead. Continue the picot edging to the next point, and then repeat this process.

Small Fluke: Coming from the back of the fabric or beadwork, push the needle through the second bead (the last bead added to the most recent picot), add a size 11 seed bead, a 4 mm bicone crystal, and three size 15 seed beads or charlottes. Turn the needle around and go through the bicone crystal, two size 11 seed beads, and in to the fabric (figure f). Turn the needle around and go back in to the last (closest) size 11 seed bead. Continue the picot edging to the next point, and then repeat this process.

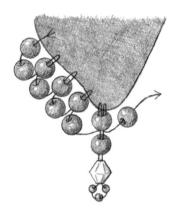

(figure f)
Stack beads at every point on the flukes.

(figure g)
Close-up of large flukes

8 Finish beading the edges of all of the large and small flukes. Add some heat-set crystals, bead stacks such as the Basic Bud and Basic Flower #1 (page 78) and micro (or no-sew) beads to embellish the flukes (figure g). Micro and no-sew beads are applied with glue. Using any tacky glue that dries clear, spread just a small amount on the flukes. Sprinkle the micro beads over the surface and press them gently with your fingers. Lift up the flukes and shake off the excess beads. Scoop the loose beads back into the micro bead container.

9 Thread a hand-sewing needle with strong thread. Place a knot in the end. Use this to close the opening of all of the flukes with a ladder stitch and hand sew all three of the large flukes to the bottom of the tail.

10 Pin the scales to the tail starting at the bottom, above the flukes. Wrap them, one at a time, around the tail in a spiral. Using strong thread, hand sew the scales as you wrap them, making sure they overlap a bit to hide the raw seams. At the top of the tail, hide the raw seam allowances with organza strips. Cut three strips from three different colors of organza, each 3" x 12" (7.6 x 30.5 cm). Use the same organza used to make organza beads (page 106). Cut some vertical slashes along one edge of the length of the strips. Light a candle and carefully seal the edges of the organza. As you run the slashed edge along the candle flame you'll see the organza shrink and create a ruffled effect. Run the straight edge of the organza along the flame to seal this edge too. With needle and thread, hand sew a gathering stitch along the straight edge of each ruffle. Hand sew the strips to the top of the tail, below the waist.

11 Three small flukes are used at the sides and back of the doll's body, at the top of the tail. Hand sew two at each side, below the organza strips. Hand sew one small fluke at the back, above the organza strips. The fourth small fluke will be used later, for the crown.

12 Above the organza at the hips, hand sew freshwater pearls and organza beads (page 106). Scatter and glue a few micro or no-sew beads along the doll's tummy. Use a heat-set crystal for the belly button.

13 Like the flukes, the wings are edged with the picot bead technique (page 28), and accent beads as done in beaded stacks (page 26). Set the wings aside.

SHELLS FOR BUST

1 Collect five colors of Delica beads, Nymo beading thread, size 10 or 12 beading needle, and beeswax. Cut 1½ yards (1.37 m) of beading thread and place this in the needle. There is no knot placed in the single end.

2 Now start peyote stitching as follows: Needle up eight white (color A) Delica beads. Take the beads toward the long end of the thread, the tail. Turn the needle back toward the tail. Add a new color A bead, skip the last bead added (bead #8), and go through #7. Add a new bead, skip #6, and go through #5. Continue this way until you have needled through #1 (figure h). (Note: Each row of the illustration is shown in a different color. Row colors do not represent a change in actual bead color.) Tie the tail and working thread together in an overhand knot. The beads can still be pulled off, but this keeps the beads tightly together. Keep the tail for now. The bead colors are changing to create the stripes of the shells on the doll's bust.

(figure h)
Lay down the base for peyote work.
Rows colored for identification only

Close-up of wings

3 Turn the needle again, heading back toward the beads you just worked. Add a new color A bead and go through the next color A up bead. Changing colors, add a color B and go through the next color A, add a color C and go through a color A. Add a color D and go through the last color A (figure i).

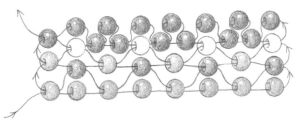

(figure i)
Work an increase over two rows.
Rows colored for identification only

4 Turn the needle again, add a color A, go through color D, add a color A, go through color C, add a color A, go through color B, add a color A, and go through a color A.

5 Increasing is a two-step process. This step is the first increase row. Turn the needle, add a color A and go through a color A, add two color B beads and go through a color A, add two color C beads and go through a color A, and add two color D beads and go through a color A.

Tip:

Watch the threads as you add the two beads. It helps to pull on the thread tightly as you go through the color A beads. When you get to the end of the row, pull on the thread tightly again. This helps keep the beads tightly together and forms the shell shape.

6 For the second increase row, turn the needle, add a color A and go through the first bead of the two color D beads, add a new color D and go through the second bead of color D, add a new color A and go through the first bead of the two color C beads, add a new color C and go through the second bead of color C, add a color A and go through the first bead of the two color B beads, add a color B and go through the second bead color B, and add a color A and go through a color A. (Note: Each row of the illustration is shown in a different color. Row colors do not represent a change in actual bead color.)

7 Turn the needle, add a color A, and go through a color A, add a color B and go through a color B, add a color B and go through a color A, add a color C and go through a color C, add a color C and go through a color A, add a color D and go through a color D, and add a color D and go through a color A.

8 Work a first increase row by adding two beads between the up colors D, C, and B.

9 Work a second increase row by following step 6.

10 Follow step 7. Repeat steps 5, 6, and 7 one more time.

11 Now you work two decrease rows by repeating step 7 twice. You will see the beads pulling in as you pull on the thread at the end of each row.

12 Repeat step 7 with two rows of color A.

13 Work the picot edging as follows: Turn the needle, add three color E beads and go into the next up color A, come out color A and add three color E beads, and take the needle into and out the next up color A. Repeat this all the way to the other side of the top of the shell. Weave the needle and thread down through several beads and do a loop knot (page 26). Cut the thread.

14 Add a starfish (below) and coral (page 105) to the bottom of the shell.

15 To attach the shell to the bust, place a knot in the end of 1 yard (0.91 m) of single thread placed in a beading needle. Attach the thread at the bottom of the bust. Pin the shell to the bust and push the needle in to a bead of the shell and come out that bead. Push the needle back in to the bust of the doll then move through the doll stuffing, over to another side of the bust, and in to the shell. Do this at the bottom and in three places along the top of the shell to secure it to the bust.

Close-up of bust with shells attached

Starfish

1 Cut 1 yard (0.91 m) of beading thread and place this in a size 12 needle. Collect two colors of Delicas (E and F) and a 3 mm bicone crystal that matches Delica color F.

2 Needle up ten Delicas of color E. Leaving a 3" (7.6 cm) tail, tie the threads together to form a circle of beads (figure j). Needle through bead #1, pulling the knot inside the bead. Add five color E beads to the needle. Skip the next bead (#2). Push the needle through bead #3. Add five more beads, skip a bead, and go into the next bead. Continue around the ten original beads in this manner. At the end you will have five picots, each with five beads. (Note: Each round of the illustration is shown in a different color. Round colors do not represent a change in actual bead color.)

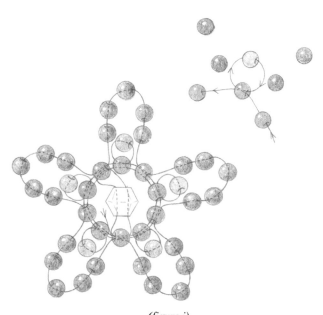

(figure j)
Make five picots around the center beads, then add an accent crystal.

Rounds colored for identification only

3 Push the needle through #1 and into the center bead between a picot (bead #2). Add a color F and go back in to #2. Push the needle through #3 to the next center bead (#4). Continue adding a color B in the center of each picot.

4 Weave the needle through the beads to an inside bead and come out that bead. Pick up the 3 mm crystal and push the needle into a bead opposite where you came out. Needle through that bead, back into the crystal, and then into the bead you came out originally, but into the other side. Going though the other side keeps the crystal from falling off.

5 Attach this starfish to the bust shell by weaving the needle and thread in and out of the beads on the shell and the beads on the starfish.

Coral (Branched Fringe)

1 Cut 1½ yards (1.37 m) of beading thread and place this in a size 10 or 12 beading needle. Weave into the bottom of the shell (see Adding Thread to Beadwork, page 26). Collect the pink size 11 seed beads, the 3 mm bicone crystals, and silver charlottes.

2 Weave the needle to the center of the shell and come out a bead at the edge. Add fifteen seed beads to the needle and thread. This is the main branch. Add a 3 mm bicone crystal and three silver charlottes. Skip the charlottes and go back through the crystal and four seed beads (figure k).

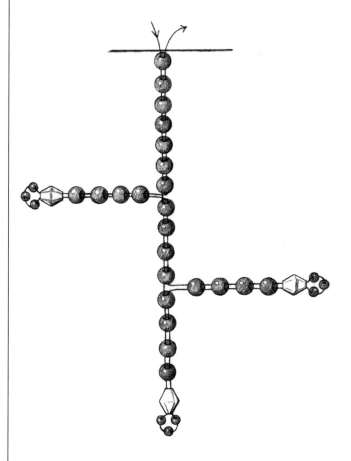

(figure k)
Add short beaded extension to basic fringe to make coral.

3 Coming out the fourth pink bead, add four new seed beads, a bicone crystal, and three charlottes. Skip the charlottes and go back in to the crystal and four pink beads. Push the needle into the main branch and, moving toward the doll, through four more pink beads.

4 Come out this bead and make another small branch with four seed beads, a bicone crystal, and three charlottes. Push the needle into the remaining pink beads on the branch.

5 Push the needle into the beads at the bottom of the shell and move over two or three beads in the shell. Create another piece of coral, but use only thirteen beads for the main branch. When that one is finished, push the needle in to the beads at the bottom of the shell and go to the other side of the center branch. Create another piece of coral with only eleven beads on the main branch.

6 After the dangling coral is completed, push the needle into the bust and come out at the top of the shell. Create coral along the top, using nine or eleven beads for the main branches. This time anchor the beads to the doll's bust.

ORGANZA BEADS

These beads can take on the look of barnacled spiral shells or they can be elegant. The results depend on what you do to make them. They are made exactly like a bead made from Tyvek. Because of the plastic fibers in both, use a dust mask and work in a well-ventilated area or outside.

1 Collect the synthetic organza, wooden skewer (satay stick), metallic thread, and embossing gun. You will also need some acrylic paint and embossing powders.

2 Cut three different colors of synthetic organza into strips that are ½" (1.3 cm) wide to no more than 2" (5 cm) long. Wrap three or four strips of varying colors, one on top of another, around the wooden skewer (figure l). Secure the strips by wrapping the bundle lightly with metallic thread that is tied in an overhand knot.

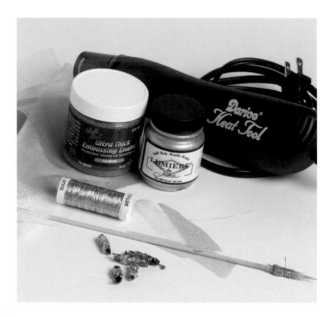

(figure l)
Organza beads in various stages of completion

3 Heat the wrapped organza with the embossing gun until you see the organza starting to melt. Watch carefully, as it heats quickly. You do not want to burn it into a glob.

4 Let the organza cool. Lightly apply a bit of paint to the bead while it is still on the skewer. Dip the damp paint into the container of embossing powder. Apply the heat gun again. The embossing powder will bubble, which lets you know the bead is finished. Quickly remove the bead from the stick. Set this aside. Create as many beads as you want.

BRACELETS

1 Free-form peyote stitch is fun and easy. It uses varying sizes of beads, for an undulating effect (figure m). (Note: Each round of the illustration is shown in a different color. Round colors do not represent a change in actual bead color.) Collect three colors of size 11 seed beads (colors A, B, and C), size 8 seed beads in the same A and B colors as the size 11 seed beads, and one color of size 15 seed beads. Cut the beading thread into a 1½ yard (1.37 m) length and thread this in a size 12 beading needle.

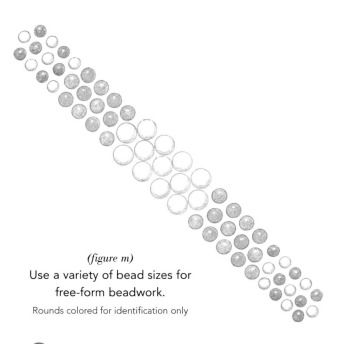

(figure m)
Use a variety of bead sizes for
free-form beadwork.

Rounds colored for identification only

2 Place seven size 15 seed beads, five size 11 in color A, five size 11 in color B, five size 8 in color A, five size 8 seed beads in color B, and five size 11 in color C. See if this fits around the mermaid's wrist. If so, you are ready to start the peyote stitching. If not, add a few more size 11 beads in color C. You'll want an even number of beads to work with.

3 Create four rows of peyote stitch beadwork (page 27), changing bead colors and sizes as you work. When finished, place the bracelet on the wrist and weave the ends together.

4 Add some freshwater pearls at the top and coral (page 105) directly to the arm. Some of the coral can hang loose.

PUTTING FRANALIZIA TOGETHER

1 Hand sew the arms to the shoulders with a hand-sewing needle and strong thread. Machine sew a running/gathering stitch down a lengthwise edge of each of two strips of organza. These strips are 2½" x 7" (6.4 x 17.8 cm) in two different colors. They are created in the same way as the organza strips at the waist (step 9 of Wings, Flukes, and Fins, page 102). Pull the threads to gather. Hand sew these at the shoulders, where the arms are sewn. At the same time, add some freshwater pearls using the bead stack technique (page 26) here and there on the doll's shoulders and bust. Add some micro (or no-sew) beads along the doll's shoulders and bust. This makes it look like she has just come out of the water. Heat-set crystals can also be added.

2 Before attaching the wings, hand sew your choice of hair (page 47) to her head. At the forehead, keep the hair behind the seam at the top of her head.

3 Bend back the open end of the fourth fluke until you have the size of crown you want. Using ladder stitches (page 28), hand sew this end to the main part of the fluke to keep its shape. Hand sew this to the doll's head, in front of the hair.

4 With a beading needle and thread, hand sew freshwater pearls, varying sizes and colors of seed beads, and shells to the forehead and sides of head. Create some branched fringe at each side of the head.

GALLERY

Loiseau

COLLEEN BABCOCK

The artist writes:

Silk cocoons gave me the inspiration to create a bird doll sitting in a nest. After making the body, I dyed her using Jacquard Dye Na Flow. I wasn't very pleased with the results, but after working on her face I decided she was okay. I loved her gentle expression and from then on she started to come together.

Dyed silk rods were wrapped around her head, which looked like a bird's crest. Her corset was woven with size 6 seed beads. After I completed it, I was surprised to see that its shape resembled the shadow of a flying bird. The underskirt was created using dyed mulberry bark. I created free-motion, machine-embroidered feathers stitched onto water-soluble stabilizer. These were attached to the mulberry bark.

The bead-embroidered wings and tail are based on a line drawing of a cardinal. I used branched and looped fringing, stacks, couching, and backstitching. Wire was used to create a frame to support the weight. The wings were created in two sections so that the wire frame could be inserted between the two. Finally, micro beads were glued to the feet and eyebrows. Each silk cocoon was edged with these beads.

Selah

ANGELA JARECKI

The artist writes:

I really enjoyed the challenge of making Selah. This pattern was a lot of fun because of the gracefulness of the figure and the three-dimensional quality of the face.

I wanted to try to make her clothing as unconventional as possible and really explore the idea of dressing her in only embellishment techniques. For the most part, her clothing is made up of ribbon, cheesecloth, and beads. All of it is hand sewn and applied directly to her body. Her legs are painted with acrylic paint in a hue that complements the ribbons and hand-dyed cheese cloth. I used seed beads and sequins for most of the beading work. Buttons and other odds and ends are used as details. Some of the sequins have a mirror finish to give her a little glitz and shine. Other sequins are transparent with a hint of color to add texture to the overall clothing effect.

For her shoes, if you can call them that, I simply wrapped her ankles and feet in sheer ribbon with added beads to give the appearance of a strap and shoe.

I named her Selah, which is a Hebrew word that means "pause, reflection," usually within the context of a prayer or psalms, because as I made her I had a chance to pause from my busy day-to-day schedule that can seem nonstop and overwhelming. This pause was a great time of reflection and thankfulness for the ability to make a doll.

Maeve of the Midnight Court

LUANNE WYKES

The artist writes:

Maeve is a fairy princess inspired by the fairies of Celtic mythology. As usual with my dolls, she let me know who she was going to be and turned out a little more benevolent in nature than the fairies who sparked her creation.

After making up body pieces from Pimatex ready-to-dye cotton, dyeing them, and painting her face, I began the process of embellishing with fabrics and beads.

Right-angle weave was used for her choker, upper arm trims, and the trim on her bodice. Decorative fringing was added to the choker and upper arm trims. The bodice trim was woven (in a string), then couched in place. Peyote stitch with picot edging was used for her wrist cuffs, belt, and headband. A drop bead was added to the center of the headband, and simple threaded bead strands each side with a flower bead toward the bottom of each strand.

One of the meanings of the word maeve is "purple flower," so she had to have a beaded flower or two. I used peyote stitch, brick stitch, and simple threaded strands of beads for stamens and stems, then attached to the lowest point of the belt.

Her tiara was made by threading beads onto beading wire, which was woven through central beads (during the threading process) and into a firm base of two strands of twisted florist wire to interlock and stabilize the whole structure.

The shoe decoration began with a cluster of simple fringing on the vamp, then the topline was edged with Patti's cuff trim. A picot was added to the tip of the toe. I wound strings of beads around the ankle and held in place with a couple of stitches. The last touch was to thread a few beads on to the wing wires before they were coiled.

Morwenna

BETH ANN WILLIAMS

The artist writes:

I loved the curvy, womanly body Patti created for this doll and I was loath to cover it up, so, I opted to make a mermaid.

The bodice treatment was created by cutting a long strip of Tyvek fabric which had been colored with Shiva oil paint sticks. I wrapped this around her body and then zapped it gently with a heat gun, causing the Tyvek to shrink and pull snugly against her body.

Three different forms of peyote stitch leaves were used in the embellishment. These were placed on her shoulder.

Her tail was made from a collage of mixed fibers, threads, Angelina, and glitter, trapped under netting and heavily machine quilted to hold it all in place. Heavy bead embroidery was used to accentuate the area where her mermaid tail joins her body. A beaded tiara completes the look.

Aging Hippie

ELINOR PEACE BAILEY

The artist writes:

What would be more fitting than to poke through the local hardware store looking for inspiration for this doll? Patti wanted "creative" beading. She knows me well, and I didn't want to disappoint her. Washers, rivets, eyelets, bearing retainers, and cotter pins all came into play. Some I covered with yarns, others I left as is. All added exactly what I wanted to give my aging hippie the desired look.

Before I finished I decided she needed a very special necklace. I carefully drilled holes in to some puzzle pieces, gave them a light wash of paint, and strung them with strong yarn.

Who said you have to use traditional glass beads to embellish a doll, or a human for that matter?

PATTERNS

BASIC DOLL BODY

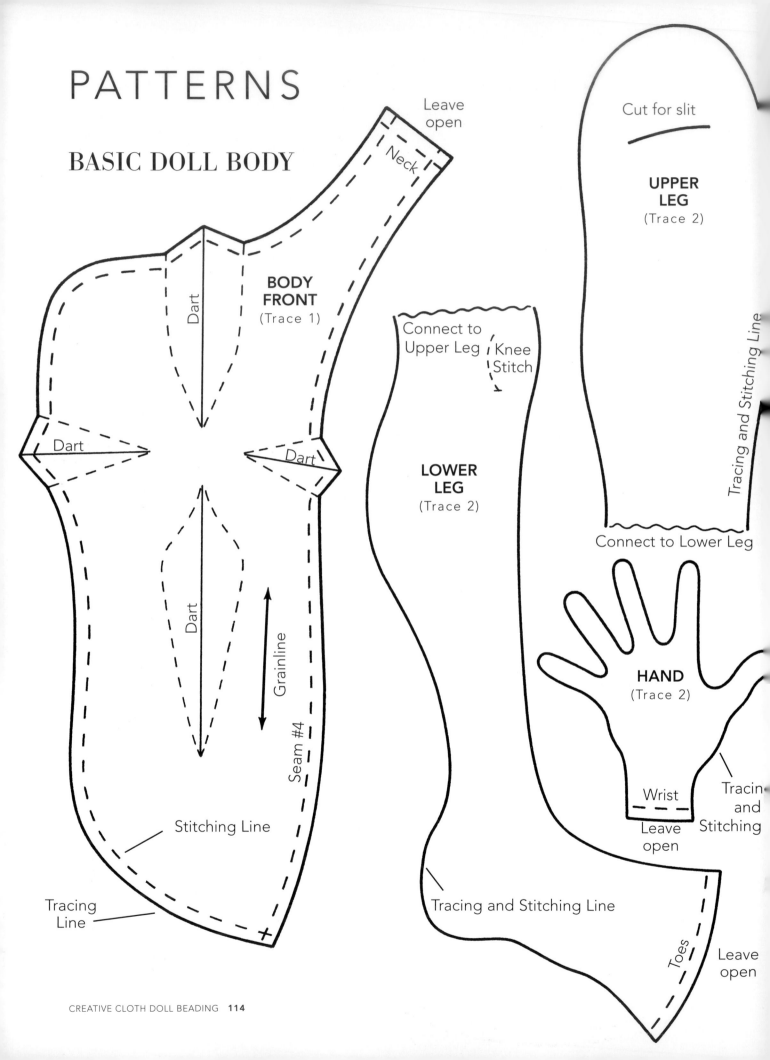

Leave open

Neck

BODY FRONT
(Trace 1)

Dart

Dart

Dart

Dart

Grainline

Seam #4

Stitching Line

Tracing Line

Connect to Upper Leg

Knee Stitch

LOWER LEG
(Trace 2)

Tracing and Stitching Line

Toes

Leave open

Cut for slit

UPPER LEG
(Trace 2)

Tracing and Stitching Line

Connect to Lower Leg

HAND
(Trace 2)

Wrist

Leave open

Tracing and Stitching

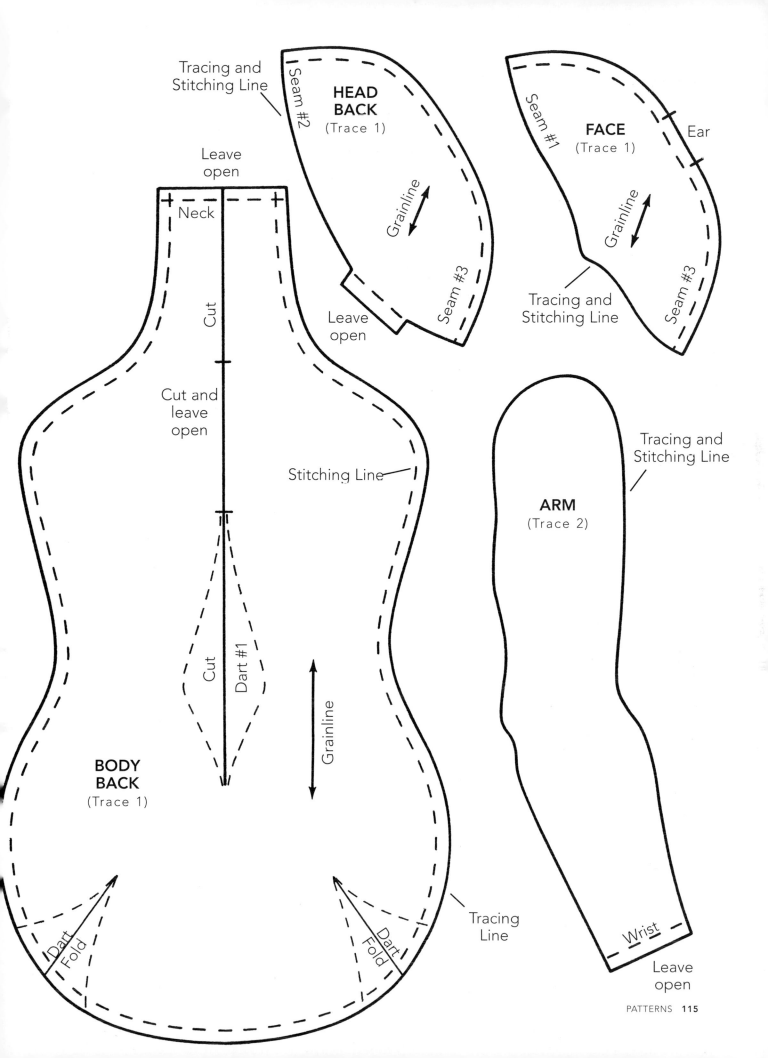

HEAD BACK
(Trace 1)

Tracing and Stitching Line

Seam #2

Leave open

Grainline

Seam #3

Leave open

FACE
(Trace 1)

Seam #1

Grainline

Ear

Seam #3

Tracing and Stitching Line

Leave open

Neck

Cut

Cut and leave open

Stitching Line

Cut

Dart #1

Grainline

BODY BACK
(Trace 1)

Dart Fold

Dart Fold

Tracing Line

ARM
(Trace 2)

Tracing and Stitching Line

Wrist

Leave open

VIVIANA

EAR
(Trace 2)

Tracing and
Stitching Line

Leave
open

WING
(Trace 2)

Wire

Wire Placement

Wire

Tracing and
Stitching Line

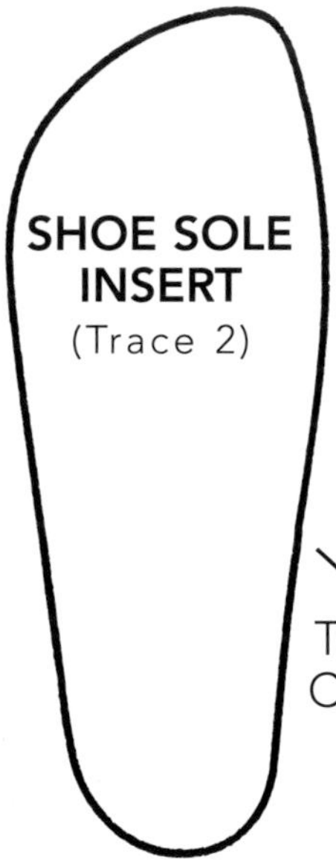

**SHOE SOLE
INSERT**
(Trace 2)

Tracing and
Cutting Line

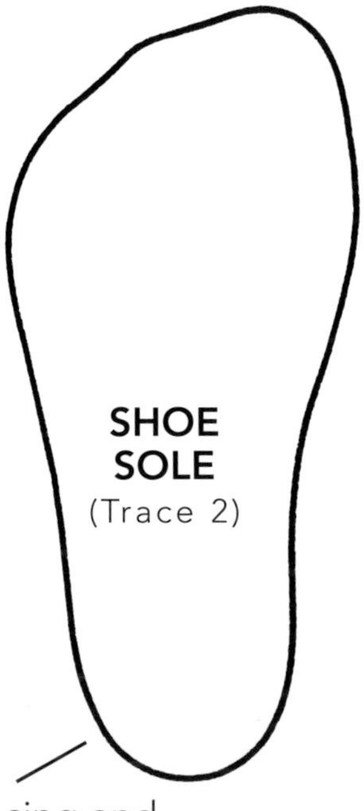

**SHOE
SOLE**
(Trace 2)

Tracing and
Stitching Line

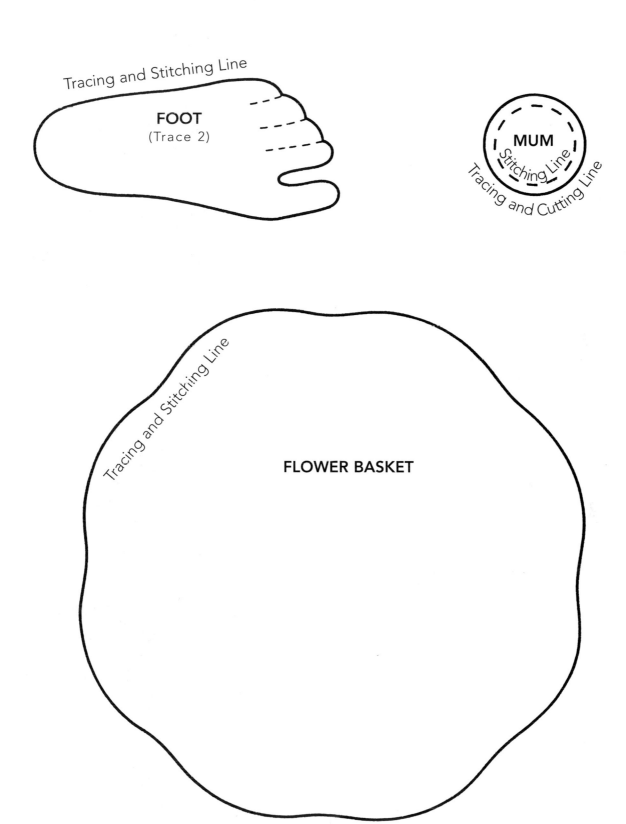

Tracing and Stitching Line

FOOT
(Trace 2)

MUM
Stitching Line
Tracing and Cutting Line

Tracing and Stitching Line

FLOWER BASKET

THE MERMAID

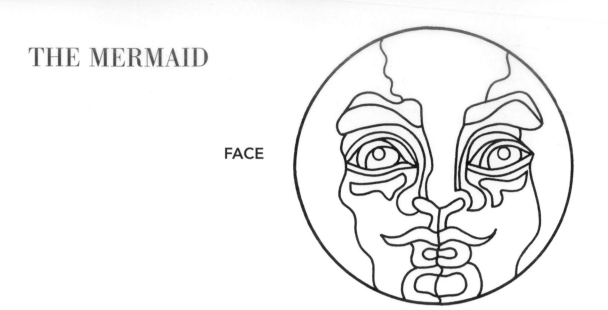

FACE

FRANALIZIA OF THE NORTH SEA

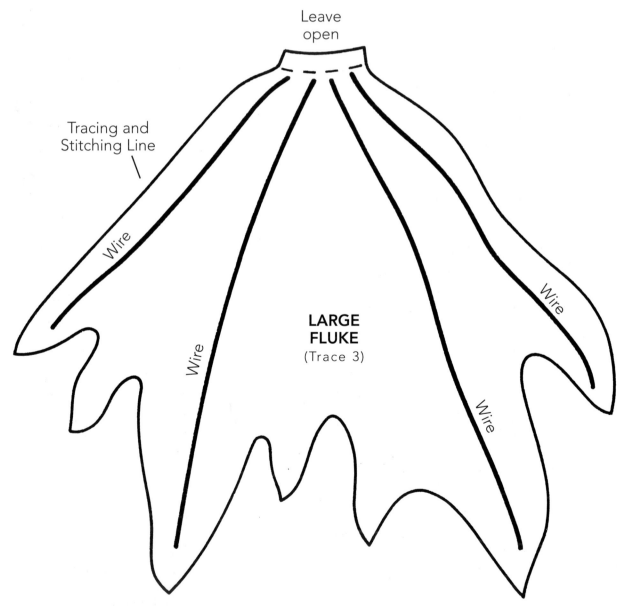

Leave
open

Tracing and
Stitching Line

Wire

Wire

Wire

Wire

**LARGE
FLUKE**
(Trace 3)

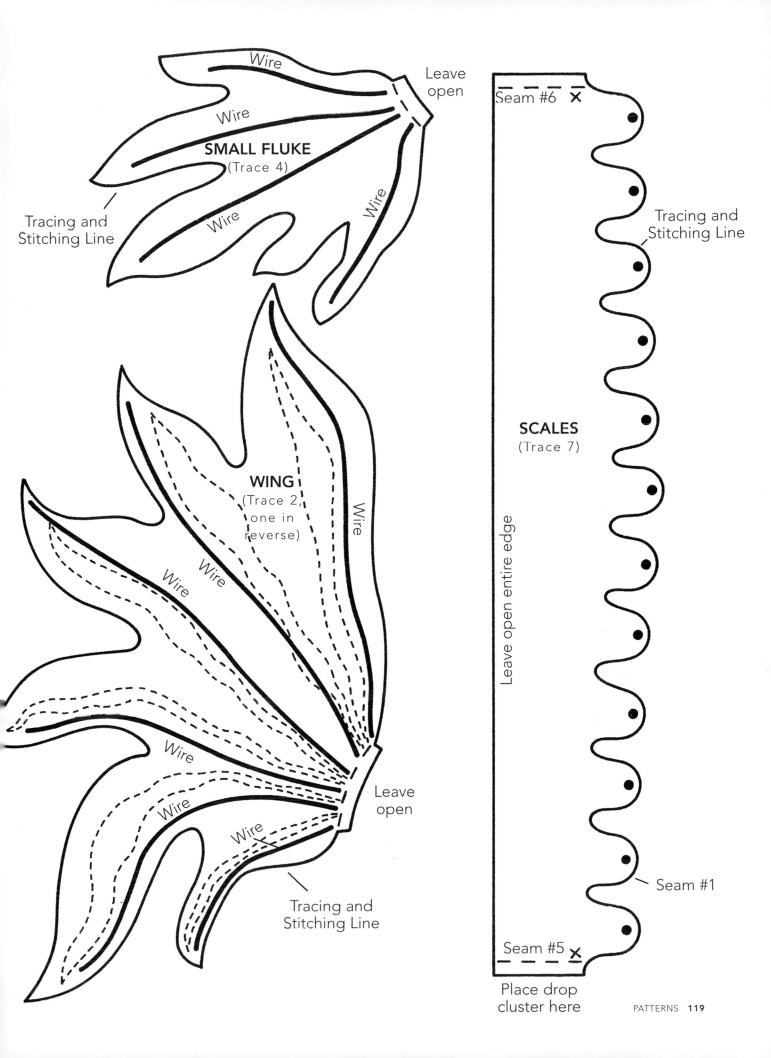

Wire

Wire

SMALL FLUKE
(Trace 4)

Wire

Wire

Wire

Leave open

Tracing and
Stitching Line

Seam #6 ✗

Tracing and
Stitching Line

SCALES
(Trace 7)

Leave open entire edge

WING
(Trace 2,
one in
reverse)

Wire

Wire

Wire

Wire

Wire

Leave
open

Wire

Tracing and
Stitching Line

Seam #1

Seam #5 ✗

Place drop
cluster here

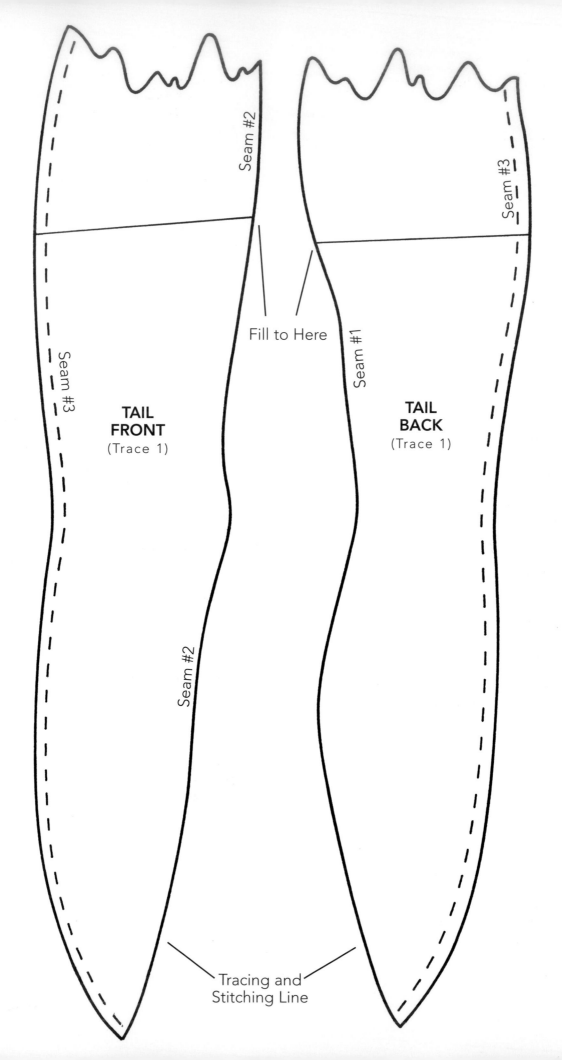

Seam #2

Seam #3

TAIL FRONT
(Trace 1)

Seam #2

Fill to Here

Seam #1

Seam #3

TAIL BACK
(Trace 1)

Tracing and
Stitching Line

RESOURCES

United States

Caravan Beads, Inc.
915 Forest Avenue
Portland, ME 04103
207.761.2503
www.caravanbeads.com
Complete line of beads, retail and wholesale

Cloth Doll Connection
www.clothdollconnection.com
Online doll-making classes, links, calendar of events

Dollmaker's Journey
www.dollmakersjourney.com
Books, patterns, and supplies for the contemporary doll artist

Fire Mountain Gems and Beads
1 Fire Mountain Way
Grants Pass, OR 97526
800.423.2319
www.firemountaingems.com
Beads, books, tools

Joggles, Inc.
www.joggles.com
Beads, books, fabrics, mohair and other fibers, patterns

Just Let Me Bead
P.O. Box 9182
Noank, CT 06340
860.245.0455
www.justletmebead.com
Bead kits, beads, classes, newsletter

Kandi Corp
P.O. Box 8345
Clearwater, FL 33758
800.985.2634
www.kandicorp.com
Heat-set crystals and Kandi Kane applicator

Meinke Toy
PMB #411, 55 E. Long Lake Road
Troy, MI 48085
www.meinketoy.com
Angelina fibers, books, stabilizers, threads

PMC Designs
9019 Stargaze Avenue
San Diego, CA 92129
858.484.5118
www.pmcdesigns.com
patti@pmcdesigns.com
Classes, heat-set crystals and applicator, newsletters, patterns, rubber stamps, tools

Quilting Arts, LLC/*Cloth Paper Scissors*
Quilting Arts Store
P.O. Box 685
Stow, MA 01775
866.698.6989
www.quiltingarts.com
Beads, books, Jacquard products, magazines, rubber stamps

Rio Grande
800.545.6566
www.riogrande.com
Large catalogue of jewelry-related supplies in all categories

Rupert, Gibbon & Spider, Inc.
P.O. Box 425
Healdsburg, CA 95448
800.442.0455
www.jacquardproducts.com
Jacquard products: Dye Na Flow, Lumiere, textile paints

Tsukineko, Inc.
17640 N.E. 65th Street
Redmond, WA 98052
425.883.7733
www.tsukineko.com
Fantastix, stamp pads

Canada

Opus Framing & Art Supplies
800.663.6953
www.opusframing.com
Books, Jacquard products, workshops

Australia

Anne's Glory Box
60 Beaumont Street
Hamilton
NSW 2303
61.2.4961.6016
www.annesglorybox.com.au
Beads, books, dyes and paints, fabrics, mohair, stabilizers

Idyll Pleasures
Shop 10 Phillip Mall
Kendall Street
West Pymble NSW 2073
61.2.9499.9335
www.idyllpleasures.com
*Beads, books, dyes and paints, doll patterns,
Jacquard products*

The Thread Studio
6 Smith Street
Perth
Western Australia 6000
61.8.9227.1561
www.thethreadstudio.com
Threads, stabilizers, paints, books, beads, online classes

New Zealand

Elna Sewing Centre and Jan's Patch
235 Moray Place, Box 5227
Dunedin
64.3.477.0611
www.elna-janspatch.co.nz
*Angelina, beads, books, fabric, paints, stabilizers,
yarns and wool*

Fabric Arts
Keriview
912 Pungaere Road, R.D. 2
Kerikeri 0295
Northland
www.fabricarts.co.nz
*Fabrics, embellishments, books and magazines,
doll patterns*

Zigzag Polymer Clay Supplies Ltd.
8 Cherry Place
Casebrook, Christchurch
64.3.359.2989
www.2dye4.co.nz
Jacquard products, Prismacolor pencils, rubber stamps

United Kingdom

Art Van Go
1 Stevenage Road
Knebworth
Herts SG3 6AN
England
44.01438.814946
www.artvango.co.uk
Books, Jacquard products, Stewart Gill paints

Crafty Notions
P.O. Box 6141
Newark NG24 2FQ
England
44.01636.700862
www.craftynotions.com
*Angelina fibers, beads and bead supplies, books, paints,
stabilizers*

Fibrecrafts and George Weil
Old Portsmouth Road
Peasmarsh, Guildford
Surrey GU3 1LZ
England
44.01483.565800
www.fibrecrafts.com
Angelina fibers, books, paints, workshops

Rainbow Silks
85 High Street
Great Missenden
Bucks HP16 OAL
England
44.01494.862111
www.rainbowsilks.co.uk
*Beads, books, classes, embossing powders and tools,
Jacquard products, rubber stamps*

Yorkshire Art Store
10 Market Place, Pickering
North Yorkshire YO18 7AA
England
44.01751.475660
www.yorkshireartstore.co.uk
*Books, embossing powders and tools, Jacquard
products, paints*

Europe

Zijdelings
Kapelstraat 93a
5046 CL Tilburg, The Hague
The Netherlands
www.zijdelings.com
Books, fabrics, Jacquard products, workshops

CONTRIBUTING BEADING ARTISTS

Lorraine Abernethy

Coromandel, New Zealand
liadolls@ihug.co.nz
www.lorrainesartdolls.com

Lorraine has designed and constructed garments for the theater and worked for designers in the fashion industry, and in retail fabrics. For the past ten years, she has drawn on her lifelong passion for fabrics and textiles and has been teaching adults screen-printing and surface design for fabrics at a variety of art schools and workshops. Lorraine has been a doll maker since 1982. She began making reproduction antique porcelain dolls back then, but after several years felt the need to return to her fabric/textile roots. Inspired by elinor peace bailey's book *Mother Plays With Dolls*, Lorraine began to design and make her own work. Lorraine now sells through galleries to collectors, conducts workshops, and designs a range of dolls for patterns. She is a full-time doll maker and is living her dream.

Colleen Babcock

London, UK
colleenbabcock@uwclub.net

Colleen has always enjoyed making things. She majored in theater design and production at York University in Toronto, Canada. This led the way to creating costumes for polymer clay dolls and now cloth dolls. Colleen finds cloth doll making magnetic because it never limits you to any one technique, material, or style. Colleen's husband, John, and parents, Barry and Kitty, are by now pros at shopping for fabric, critiquing dolls, and stoking the creative fires.

elinor peace bailey

Little Old Lady Originals
Vancouver, WA
USA
epbdolls@aol.com
www.epbdolls.com

elinor peace bailey received her art education through Parsons School of Design, Tyler School of Arts, and Brigham Young University. She has written *Mother Plays With Dolls, The Rag Doll: From Plain to Fancy*, and recently, *Two Doll Makers Meet in the Middle*, published by Krause. She has self-published sixty-five doll patterns and seven books about doll making from the simple to the complex. She has illustrated books for Bernina of America and Fairfield Processing, and has designed fabric for P&B Textiles, Daisy Kingdom, and Concord Fabrics. She has acted as consultant for *Crafts* magazine, Prym Dritz Corp. (which has manufactured her dolls), Fairfield Processing, and Springs Mills. She is a writer of not truly bad poetry, and she sings with great energy. She presently is experimenting with journaling and altered books, in addition to creating art to wear, which she shows off by wearing herself. She has enjoyed great kindness from her friends and audiences wherever she has gone and, therefore, she plans to continue her art career.

Judy Brown

Twinsburg, OH
USA
brownth@aol.com

Judy Brown has always loved sewing, painting, and creating. Doll making is the perfect outlet for her as it combines her passion for sewing, painting, sculpting, and beading. She majored in art at Kent State University where she met and married her husband, Tom. Tom's army career enabled Judy and their three daughters to move around the country. While living in St. Louis in 1990, she founded her company, Make Believe. In 1994, the family moved to Virginia where Judy enrolled in an elinor peace bailey class and immediately became enthralled with cloth doll making. Her business and talents shifted to this facet of doll making, which quickly became her creative focus. She currently resides in Twinsburg, Ohio, and teaches doll making at several local quilt shops. She is a member of two cloth doll clubs and recently won a first-place ribbon for her doll in the Lake Farmpark quilt show.

Jenny Campbell

Victoria, Australia
acjc6@bigpond.com

Jenny is a primary school teacher who has always loved sewing and creating. She designs and makes clothes for herself and her family. She is intrigued by all types of crafts, but patchwork was the craft she embraced seriously for many years. The progression to making artistic dolls seemed quite natural. Jenny was at a quilting day and met a woman who had a wonderful book showing pictures of dolls created by American doll artists. She was hooked on the craft and found she was able to use all the leftover bits from her quilts. She found several doll groups on the Internet and has been making and experimenting with cloth and polymer clay dolls ever since. She beads and experiments with all types of fabric to create new and unusual pieces. Jenny's latest venture has been making lampwork beads and altered books. She loves to attend workshops and learn different techniques—always looking at how she can simplify the process for children. Jenny teaches art as well as Asian and environmental studies with a focus on Indonesia. Jenny lives with her husband, Alan, in their house in the Australian bush with their two dogs, lots of kangaroos, wallabies, and birds. Their two children are grown. Their son, Ben, is married and they are to be grandparents very soon. Their daughter, Anna, is doing what most young folks do these days—working and having fun around the world.

Mary Connolly
Victoria, Australia
marypatricia13@yahoo.com

Though born in Gippsland in a little town called Trafalgar, Mary and her family moved to Geelong, where she met and married her husband forty-two years ago. They have four adult children and six grandchildren. Being the eldest of twelve children without much money, Mary started to make her own clothes at the age of ten. When she married, she made all her own and her children's clothes and also cloth toys and dolls. Mary first saw different cloth dolls when she was on holiday in Bendigo and went to an exhibition by the Good Time Girls Cloth Doll Club. She was blown away by the wonderful dolls and immediately joined their club. Her first workshop was with Patti Culea about seven years ago. A few months later, she was introduced to Kathy Williams and Elaine Mitchell who were starting a doll club called Trolly Dolly Cloth Doll Club of Geelong. Since then Mary has attended many workshops and made many dolls and is learning new things every day.

Vera Evans
North Olmsted, OH
USA
veraevans@adelphia.net

Vera lives in northwestern Ohio with her husband, Bill, and their two children. Her passion for dolls began about ten years ago. She had taken a class with elinor peace bailey and met other people who shared the same interests. Beading began as just another embellishment technique for dolls but soon became an obsession. She is never without her beads and frequently takes beading classes to learn new techniques. The jewelry she creates is sold locally and when the time is available she also teaches. The best of both worlds collide when she can combine beading with doll making.

Kathryn Howat-Flintoff
Te Awamutu, New Zealand
flinthowat@xtra.co.nz

Kathryn has had a love of sewing, arts, and crafts since childhood, making her first garment at the age of ten. Her creativity has gathered momentum since then, resulting in a serious addiction (of absolutely the best kind) to cloth doll making, patchwork/quilting, and machine embroidery. She is largely self-taught, but has in later years been able to attend conferences, tutorials, and classes, and has gathered valuable techniques, tips, and good friends. Books and magazines have also enabled her to broaden her outlook. Kathryn is currently designing her own cloth dolls. She lives in rural Waikato on the North Island of New Zealand, on a dairy farm with her husband. They are building a new house and have incorporated a specifically designed studio to support her habit and some teaching.

Angela Jarecki
Blue Springs, MO
USA
whimsymoondesigns@yahoo.com

Angela Jarecki was a greeting card artist with Hallmark Cards for ten years. She now freelances for them and other card and publishing companies. She had rooms full of creative "stuff" in her stash but no way to put it to use until about five years ago when she landed on the fantastic planet of doll making. With her lifelong love for dolls, she was able to find a way to use her fibers, fabrics, yarn, beads, and embellishments in a marvelous way. Today, she helps others discover their creative talent by teaching art classes for children, adult workshops, and several Internet classes on making dolls. Angela, her husband and four children make their home outside of Kansas City, Missouri.

Valérie LeGrand-Preney
Sens, France
thread_embroidery@yahoo.fr

Valérie lives in Burgundy, France, with her four children and husband. Sewing, creative embroidery, fiber art, and mixed media are a very important part of her life. In 2003, she discovered an incredible new world—creative dolls. Since then, she combines all techniques and materials with her passion for colors, textures, and textiles when creating dolls. She also constructs models to express her ideas. Valérie received first place in the 2005 Sulky Challenge Amateur Doll Category.

Jill Maas

Wanganui, New Zealand
gordon.maas@clear.net.nz

Jill lives in Wanganui in the North Island of New Zealand. Her love of fabrics, color, and "encouragement" at the right time led her to creating soft sculptures for family and friends. Jill is a well-known doll designer and artist. She teaches throughout New Zealand and Australia. Her patterns are sold in New Zealand, Australia, the UK, and the United States. Jill's company name, Slightly Weathered Ladies and More, is just that—slightly weathered, but not downtrodden. Attitude, a sense of humor, and great respect are keys to survival.

Teresa Malyon

Clacton on Sea, Essex, UK
teresamalyon@aol.com
www.splendorincloth.co.uk

Teresa comes from the porcelain doll world. She's won awards many times for her exquisite dolls. Her specialty is sculpting babies. During breaks from sculpting wee ones she makes cloth dolls. She conducts workshops in her lovely home bringing in tutors from around the globe. She loves sharing the doll world with as many people as she can.

Sharon Mann

Las Vegas, NV
USA
smann45333@aol.com
www.sharonmanndesigns.com

Sharon's passion is to design with needle, thread, and yarn. She infuses her love of traditional needlecraft with other craft techniques to produce dimensional and novel projects. Sharon is a published designer and currently her artistic endeavors include fiber arts, crochet, knitting, and embellishment beading.

Di McDonald

Palmerston North, New Zealand
di@dyzee.com
www.dyzee.com

Di has moved back to the place of her birth, New Zealand, to be nearer to her family. She is recently married for the second time, and her new husband is very supportive of her creative work. Her background is in fashion design and manufacturing. She enjoys working with fiber and paper and, although her main focus has been on doll design, she has branched out to all mixed-media work and visual journaling. Di loves to teach and connect with other like-minded women and wonderful creative friends she has made through her website and doll making.

Michelle Meinhold

Fresno, CA
USA
meinhold@csufresno.edu
www.michellemeinhold.com

Michelle has been playing with beads for as long as she can remember. She started collecting beads at an early age and her collection has grown from there. Beading was once used to embellish the cloth dolls she made, but the lure of making wearable art out of the beads was just as tempting. Now, Michelle's medium of choice is Swarovski crystals, both new and vintage. To feed her habit, she teaches beading around the United States.

Wendy Ness

Mount Compass, South Australia, Australia
nyowee@ozemail.com.au

Wendy is not a doll artist (she has only made about twelve dolls so far), nor is she a beader. Instead, she is a decorative painter who happens to love dolls, fabric, painting, and art journals. Texture, color, and good design drive everything she creates, but she is also a great believer in "less is more," allowing the work to tell her when it is finished. Wendy lives on a dairy farm with her wonderful husband and has two grown children who no longer live at home. Wendy could be the eternal student if she had the opportunity, but she also learns a lot through students who attend her painting workshops. Wendy loves sharing ideas, techniques, and happy times with other creative people and feels hugely rewarded if that process inspires others to greater things.

Kandra J. Norsigian

Kandra's Beads
Arroyo Grande, CA
USA
kandra@kandrasbeads.com
www.kandrasbeads.com

Kandra has always loved working with her hands. Whether cooking or beading, she is most satisfied when making things. Owning a bead shop and teaching beading techniques has helped Kandra explore a number of mediums. Besides working with seed beads, Kandra has done lampworking and kiln glass making, gourd arts, quilting, felting, metal clay, enameling, wire work, embroidery, weaving, polymer clay, and doll making. Her work is strongly informed by her love of color in both the natural and man-made worlds, and by shapes, especially the spiral and gingko leaf. She believes that creative expression is about play. When working with her hands in any medium, the "child" inside gets to come out. In this way, she nurtures herself and finds a peaceful place in the world.

Beth Ann Williams
Grand Rapids, MI
USA
bawill@sprynet.com
www.bethannwilliams.com

Beth Ann has been rather passionately obsessed with cloth dolls and figurative art since her first encounter with a special exhibit of art dolls at a national quilt show in 2004. However, she is probably best known for her longer career as a contemporary quilt, fiber, and mixed-media artist. Her award-winning work has appeared in museums, galleries, books, magazines, and calendars. She is a three-time author, and has been a featured guest on the Home & Garden and DIY television networks. She exhibits, lectures, and teaches a variety of fabric and surface design workshops and classes across the country. Currently, she is serving as the president of the West Michigan Quilters' Guild. Since 1990, she has made her home in Grand Rapids, Michigan, with her husband, John, and daughters, Caryl and Connor.

Luanne Wykes
Traralgon, Victoria, Australia
luanne@luannewykes.com
www.luannewykes.com

Luanne is a self-taught multimedia artist, best known for her decorative art. She has dabbled in most fields of the art and handicraft world since childhood. Her cloth doll journey began in 1998, when her daughter was diagnosed with Type 1 diabetes at eight years of age. Cloth dolls, new to Luanne at the time, became a coping device and wonderful therapy, and still are to this day. She uses her painting skills in doll making, particularly in the creation of unique faces. In fact, cloth dolls combine all of Luanne's creative passions in one package. She is a popular and sought-after designer and teacher for her innovative techniques and original work. Her designs have been published in many magazines and books.

FURTHER READING

The Beaded Garden
Diane Fitzgerald, Interweave Press
ISBN 1-931499-55-1

Beading with Peyote Stitch
Jeannette Cook and Vicki Star, Interweave Press
ISBN 1-883010-71-3

Creative Cloth Doll Couture
Patti Medaris Culea, Quarry Books
ISBN 1-59253-217-9

Creative Cloth Doll Faces
Patti Medaris Culea, Quarry Books
ISBN 1-59253-144-X

Creative Cloth Doll Making
Patti Medaris Culea, Rockport Publishers
ISBN 1-56496-942-8

ABOUT THE AUTHORS

Patti Medaris Culea came to the doll world via the fine arts world. She found that her training and artistic skills have helped her in her doll designs and classes she teaches. She began painting portraits in oils and pastels. While living in Japan she studied the art of *kumihimo* (Japanese braiding using a marudai and bobbins). This piqued her interest in fibers. After returning to the United States, she studied soft sculpture using nylon stockings, but she wanted something a bit sturdier so she could use her painting skills. She found some cloth doll designers who were exciting to her and studied with them. In 1991, she started developing her own style of doll making and has been creating the human figure in cloth ever since.

In demand as a teacher, Patti travels throughout the world spreading the joy of cloth doll making. Her work has been featured in magazines such as *Dolls, Bears and Collectables* in Australia; *Stitch* and *Doll* magazines in the UK; *Soft Dolls & Animals!, Art Doll Quarterly, Cloth Paper Scissors*, and *Quilting Arts Magazine* in the United States. You can also see her work in several books: *Angel Crafts* by Holly Harrison, *Fabric Art Journals* by Pam Sussman (both by Quarry Books), and her own books, *Creative Cloth Doll Making, Creative Cloth Doll Faces*, and *Creative Cloth Doll Couture*, also published by Quarry Books.

San Diego, CA
USA
patti@pmcdesigns.com
www.pmcdesigns.com

Anne Hesse is a widely renowned doll artist and workshop instructor both nationally and internationally. Anne's work can be seen in Susanna Oroyan's books *Anatomy of a Doll, Designing the Doll*, and *Finishing the Doll*, and Martha Le Van's *Making Creative Cloth Dolls*. Anne has been featured in two of Patti Culea's previous books with Quarry Books, and she was the featured doll artist in the Spring 2006 issue of *Art Doll Quarterly*. She has been commissioned to create original dolls for television and film, and has twice been invited to participate in the White House Christmas Collection of American artists.

Richmond, KY
USA
annie@adelphia.net
www.anniedolls.com

Laura McCabe is a primarily self-taught beadweaver with an education in historical costume reproduction and restoration, and anthropology. She produces elaborately beaded body adornment that combines Native American, African Zulu, and Victorian bead-weaving techniques with modern materials and color schemes. She exhibits her work in national and international beadwork exhibitions and sells her finished work at boutiques and galleries throughout the United States, as well as through her website, www.lauramccabejewelry.com. She maintains a working studio in Mystic, Connecticut, and teaches beading workshops in the US and internationally.

Noank, CT
USA
info@justletmebead.com
www.justletmebead.com

ACKNOWLEDGMENTS

A few years ago when I completed my first book, it was a dream come true. Now that the fourth has been published, all I can say is, "Don't wake me because I need some sleep!" Seriously, I'm still amazed with and blessed by all the support I have received during these adventures from family, friends, contributing artists, and my editors.

During the creation of this book, I often felt more like a student than an author. Beading is much more involved than other doll-making techniques. Thank you, Anne Hesse and Laura McCabe, who accepted my offer to work on a book together. It was Laura who taught me about crystals, and Anne who instilled a love for bead embroidery.

Thank you to my parents for their help with the mermaid. I was having all sorts of trouble designing the tail when my mom came up with the scale idea. Mom passed away before the book went to print; however, she's now looking down from heaven and I know she loves the way the doll turned out. I owe so much to my parents. Mom probably got tired of me telling her that, and Dad hears it every day.

The fingerprints of my family are on this book, as has been the case with the others. You'll probably detect word magic on some of the text from my husband, John. While I was going "beady-eyed" with the book and away on teaching trips, the fort was held, orders on my website were filled, and the everyday household chores were done. Thank you for understanding and for all of the "Welcome home Patti" signs on the lawn.

Thanks to Heidi, our daughter, for helping edit the contributors' descriptions and bios. Although she had her hands full teaching fifth-graders in Brussels, she was a great help over there and when she came home for the summer.

Encouragement also came from our oldest daughter, JB (who made a doll for my first book). She was busy with her two-year-old daughter and was expecting another daughter about the time this book got its final approval.

Speaking of final approval, a huge thanks to Mary Ann Hall for asking me to do another book. I so appreciate your patience when I needed time off due to caring for my mother and then being with my father after her passing.

I'm deeply grateful to each of my contributing artist friends. All of your work was outstanding and so creative. After spending what seemed like half my life beading the mermaid, I think if we tallied all the hours spent just in beading, we'd need a time-out to console each other. However, we know we aren't rewarded for time spent; it's doing what we love and helping others learn the joys of doll making and, in this instance, creative beading. All of you will bring great happiness to people who will see what you've done.

Finally, to those who read this book, I thank you for joining us in this special world of art. Beads are part of a community, and artists are all connected on a string. Enjoy every technique explored in this book and let's remember to hang together. God bless you all.